olive

100 of the very best
CHICKEN RECIPES

olive

100 of the very best
CHICKEN RECIPES

olive *magazine*

Copyright © Immediate Media Company London Limited 2016

The right of Immediate Media Co. to be identified as the author
of this work has been asserted in accordance with the
Copyright, Designs and Patents Act 1988.

This edition first published in Great Britain in 2016 by
Orion, an imprint of the Orion Publishing Group Ltd
Carmelite House
50 Victoria Embankment
London, EC4Y 0DZ
An Hachette UK Company

10 9 8 7 6 5 4 3 2 1

A CIP catalogue record for this book is available
from the British Library.

ISBN: 978 1 4091 6226 1

Designed by Goldust Design

Printed in China

The Orion Publishing Group's policy is to use papers that are natural, renewable and recyclable
and made from wood grown in sustainable forests. The logging and manufacturing processes are
expected to conform to the environmental regulations of the country of origin.

Every effort has been made to fulfil requirements with regard to reproducing copyright material.
The author and publisher will be glad to rec

www.orionbooks.co.uk

For more recipes visit olivemagazine.com

Contents

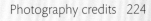

Introduction

olive is Britain's brightest food magazine. More than just a collection of recipes, it's about sharing the good stuff; cooking for family and friends, discovering great restaurants and enjoying weekends away. Upmarket and glossy, our recipe photography is the best in the market. In print and online at olivemagazine.com, we keep our audience up-to-date with new food trends and provide imaginative recipes for weeknights and weekends.

We are consuming more chicken than ever before and who can blame us? It is easy to cook, low in fat and delicious in any type of dish. In *100 of the Very Best Chicken Recipes*, we have put together a collection of our best chicken recipes. Every recipe includes our trademark photography, so you know exactly what you are aiming for. From a lazy Sunday slow-roast chicken, butter chicken curry to our famous chicken cacciatore, this is the only collection of chicken recipes you will need.

At **olive**, we believe you can eat well at home even if you don't have bags of time. Most of the recipes in this book are quick and easy, and can be made using easily accessible ingredients and equipment found in your kitchen. We think weekends are for more adventurous cooking so we have also included some recipes that will take more time, but will be oh so worth it.

Notes and conversion tables

There are three categories of recipes throughout the **olive** books.

Easy: Most of our recipes come under this category and are very simple to put together with easy-to-find ingredients.

A little effort: These recipes require either more time, shopping for harder-to-find ingredients or a little more complicated cooking techniques.

Tricky but worth it: We have offered a few recipes that fall under this category and require a higher level of skill and concentration. These recipes give readers an occasional challenge but the little extra effort is always well worth the reward.

- Recipe timings are based on the total amount of time needed to finish the recipe so includes both prep and cook time.
- Provenance matters to us. Where possible, we use free-range eggs and chickens, humanely reared meat, organic dairy products, sustainably caught fish, unrefined sugar and fairly traded ingredients.
- Nutritional information is provided for all recipes. Because *olive* recipes don't always give exact quantities for ingredients such as oil and butter, nutritional quantities may not always be 100 per cent accurate. Analysis includes only the listed ingredients, not optional ingredients, such as salt, or any serving suggestions.
- Care should be taken when buying meat that you intend to eat raw or rare.
- Our recipes use large eggs, unless otherwise stated. Pregnant women, the elderly, babies and toddlers, and people who are unwell should avoid eating raw and partially cooked eggs.
- Vegetarians should always check the labels on shop-bought ingredients such as yoghurt, cheese, pesto and curry sauces, to ensure they are suitable for vegetarian consumption.
- Unless otherwise specified, if oil is listed as an ingredient, any flavourless oil such as groundnut, vegetable or sunflower oil can be used.

Liquid measurements

Metric	Imperial	Australian	US
25ml	1fl oz		
60ml	2fl oz	¼ cup	¼ cup
75ml	3fl oz		
100ml	3½fl oz		
120ml	4fl oz	½ cup	½ cup
150ml	5fl oz		
180ml	6fl oz	¾ cup	¾ cup
200ml	7fl oz		
250ml	9fl oz	1 cup	1 cup
300ml	10½fl oz	1¼ cups	1¼ cups
350ml	12½fl oz	1½ cups	1½ cups
400ml	14fl oz	1¾ cups	1¾ cups
450ml	16fl oz	2 cups	2 cups
600ml	1 pint	2½ cups	2½ cups
750ml	1¼ pints	3 cups	3 cups
900ml	1½ pints	3½ cups	3½ cups
1 litre	1¾ pints	1 quart or 4 cups	1 quart or 4 cups
1.2 litres	2 pints		
1.4 litres	2½ pints		
1.5 litres	2¾ pints		
1.7 litres	3 pints		
2 litres	3½ pints		

Oven temperature guide

	Electricity			Gas
	°C	°F	(fan) °C	Mark
Very cool	110	225	90	¼
	120	250	100	½
Cool	140	275	120	1
	150	300	130	2
Moderate	160	325	140	3
	170	350	160	4½
Moderately hot	190	375	170	5
	200	400	180	6
Hot	220	425	200	7
	230	450	210	8
Very hot	240	475	220	9

Light and
healthy

Shirataki noodles with poached miso ginger chicken broth

30 minutes | serves 4 | easy

1 litre light chicken stock
5cm piece of root ginger, sliced
2 skinless chicken breasts
4 baby pak choi, halved
2 tbsp white miso
1 tsp sesame oil
300g shirataki noodles, rinsed thoroughly and drained
¼ bunch of chives, chopped, to serve
salt and freshly ground black pepper

Shirataki noodles are low in carbs and calories, and will satisfy your appetite without busting your daily cal and carb intake. You'll often find them packed in water, and they can have a peculiar smell when opened, so give them a good rinse before using.

Put the chicken stock in a saucepan with the ginger, bring to a simmer and cook gently for 5 minutes. Add the chicken breasts and poach for 10 minutes, or until cooked through, then remove and set them aside to rest. Cook the pak choi in the stock for 4 minutes, then remove and set aside.

Strain the broth into a clean saucepan. Add the miso and sesame oil and bring back to a gentle simmer. Slice the chicken and divide it between 4 bowls with the noodles and pak choi. Spoon over the hot broth, season and serve sprinkled with chives.

Per serving 147 kcals, **protein** 25.6g, **carbohydrate** 3.7g, **fat** 2.6g, **saturated fat** 0.7g, **fibre** 3.2g, **salt** 1.7g

Poached chicken with vegetable and orzo broth

30 minutes | serves 4 | easy

1 litre chicken stock
2 skinless chicken breasts
4 carrots, peeled and thinly
   sliced
100g orzo
¼ Savoy cabbage, cored
   and roughly sliced
3 spring onions, sliced
2 tbsp pesto
salt and freshly ground
   black pepper

Easy to make and very light and healthy, this soup is perfect all year round.

Put the stock, chicken and carrots in a large saucepan. Bring to the boil, then turn down the heat and simmer for 5 minutes. Add the orzo, cabbage, spring onions and season. Simmer for another 5 minutes, until the orzo is tender and the chicken cooked.

Remove the chicken from the broth and cut it into thin slices. Ladle the vegetables, orzo and broth into bowls before topping with chicken slices and spooning over the pesto.

Per serving 250 kcals, **protein** 22.5g, **carbohydrate** 27.5g, **fat** 6.4g, **saturated fat** 1.7g, **fibre** 3.6g, **salt** 2.19g

Spring chicken salad

30 minutes | serves 4 | easy

2 skinless chicken breasts
100ml white wine
200ml cold water
1 small onion, halved
3–4 sprigs of thyme
1 bay leaf
6 black peppercorns
150g small broad beans
16 baby carrots, trimmed
1 small fennel bulb,
    trimmed
small handful of chives
5–6 sprigs of tarragon,
    leaves stripped
1 level tbsp small capers,
    rinsed and drained
handful of curly parsley,
    roughly chopped
salt and freshly ground
    black pepper

For the vinaigrette
2 tsp white wine vinegar
juice of ½ lemon
1 garlic clove, peeled and
    finely chopped
2 tsp Dijon mustard
1½ tsp golden caster sugar
½ tsp flaked sea salt
3 tbsp olive oil

Make the most of seasonal spring veg with this fresh, light salad. Poached chicken is tossed with carrots, fennel, broad beans and chives and a mustardy, herby vinaigrette.

Put the chicken breasts in a saucepan and pour over the wine. Add the water, onion, thyme, bay leaf and peppercorns. Place the pan over a medium heat, cover and bring to a gentle simmer. Poach the chicken for 10 minutes.

Strain the chicken and liquor through a fine sieve, reserving the stock. Set the chicken on a chopping board to cool and pour the stock into a clean saucepan. Pod the beans and bring the stock to the boil, add the beans and return to the boil and cook for 2 minutes. Remove the beans with a slotted spoon and refresh them in a sieve under cold running water until cool, then drain them. Cook the carrots in the stock for 5 minutes. Refresh and drain them too.

Squeeze all the beans out of their skins and put them in a large serving bowl. Add the carrots. Cut the fennel into wafer-thin slices. Add it to the bowl along with the whole chives, tarragon leaves and capers. Scatter in the parsley.

Tear the chicken into long shreds and scatter it over the salad. Whisk together all the vinaigrette ingredients, except the oil, with some black pepper in a small bowl. Whisk in the oil a little at a time until thickened. Season the salad, then drizzle over the vinaigrette and toss lightly before serving.

Per serving 225 kcals, **protein** 20.5g, **carbohydrate** 11.9g, **fat** 10.1g, **saturated fat** 1.4g, **fibre** 5g, **salt** 1.2g

Dijon mustard and honey glazed chicken and watercress salad

30 minutes | serves 2 | easy

1 tbsp Dijon mustard,
  plus 1 tsp
1 tbsp runny honey,
  plus 1 tsp
1 tbsp extra-virgin olive oil,
  plus extra for drizzling
2 skinless chicken breasts
1 tbsp white wine vinegar
100g watercress
½ small red onion, finely
  sliced
½ cucumber, halved
  lengthways, seeds
  removed and sliced
salt and freshly ground
  black pepper

Light and refreshing, this salad requires few ingredients and can be whipped up in no time for a dinner party starter or a main meal.

Mix 1 tablespoon of the mustard with 1 tablespoon of the honey and a drizzle of oil in a bowl, and season. Spread the mixture all over the chicken.

Heat a griddle or heavy-based frying pan until hot. Griddle or fry the chicken for about 7 minutes on each side, or until cooked through. Remove from the pan and leave to rest for 5 minutes, then slice at an angle. Mix the vinegar with the olive oil and the remaining mustard and honey, and season. Toss the chicken with the watercress, red onion, cucumber and dressing, and serve.

Per serving 288 kcals, **protein** 33.4g, **carbohydrates** 15.4g, **fat** 10g, **saturated fat** 1.6g, **fibre** 1.7g, **salt** 1.2g

Sumac spice-crusted chicken and green bean salad with spiced yoghurt dressing

40 minutes | serves 4–6 | easy

4 skinless chicken breasts
1 tbsp extra-virgin olive oil
3 tsp chilli flakes
3 tsp sumac
1 tsp ground cinnamon
2 tsp ground cumin
40g pine nuts
salt and freshly ground
  black pepper

For the yoghurt dressing
100g natural yoghurt
2 tbsp milk
2 tbsp white wine vinegar
grated zest and juice of
  1 lemon
1 tbsp chopped dill
½ garlic clove, crushed

For the salad
300g green beans,
  trimmed and some
  halved lengthways
1 small red onion, cut into
  half moons
1 tsp sumac
a few dill fronds, chopped
seeds of 1 pomegranate,
  or a 100g tub of seeds
1 purple or orange carrot,
  cut into ribbons

This sumac spice-crusted chicken and green bean salad looks fantastic as it is bursting with colour and is packed with flavour too. What's even better is that it comes in at under 500 calories – it's the perfect summer salad.

Preheat the oven to 210°C/Fan 190°C/Gas 6½. Rub the chicken with the olive oil and season well. Mix the chilli flakes, sumac, cinnamon and cumin together, then roll the chicken in the spices. Put the chicken onto a baking tray and roast it for 20 minutes, or until the chicken is tender and cooked through. During the last 4 minutes of the cooking time, sprinkle the pine nuts over the top. Remove the chicken from the oven and set aside to cool.

Mix the ingredients for the dressing in a small bowl and set it aside.

For the salad, cook the beans for 1 minute in salted water, drain and refresh in cold water. Dry the beans and arrange them on a serving platter. Mix the onion with the sumac and spread them over the beans. Top with the dill, pomegranate seeds and carrot ribbons. When the chicken has cooled, slice it and arrange it over the vegetables with the pine nuts. Serve with the dressing to pour over.

Per serving 370 kcals, **protein** 37.5g, **carbohydrate** 18.3g, **fat** 14.8g, **saturated fat** 2g, **fibre** 6.7g, **salt** 0.6g

Herb, basmati and chicken salad

25 minutes | serves 4 | easy

150g basmati rice
1 tbsp olive oil
2 onions, halved and sliced
300g frozen peas
grated zest and juice of
  1 lemon
2 cooked skinless chicken
  breasts, torn into
  bite-sized pieces
large handful of basil,
  chopped
large handful of dill,
  chopped
salt and freshly ground
  black pepper
lemon wedges, to serve

The dill and lemon in this light, easy salad complement each other perfectly. Serve warm as a light dinner or cold the next day.

Cook the rice according to the packet instructions. Heat the oil in a frying pan then tip in the onions and season. Cook for about 15 minutes, until completely soft and golden. You can turn up the heat at the end to give them a final browning.

Meanwhile, boil the peas until just tender, rinse under very cold running water, drain and put them in a large serving bowl. Add the lemon zest and juice. Tip in the cooked rice and stir. Add the chicken and a third of the browned onions then toss to combine. Stir in the herbs and season before topping with the remaining onions. Squeeze over a lemon wedge and serve.

Per serving 317 kcals, **protein** 26.7g, **carbohydrate** 39.7g, **fat** 6.8g, **saturated fat** 1.6g, **fibre** 5.8g, **salt** 0.15g

Satay chicken with peanut sauce

30 minutes | serves 2 | easy

4 skinless, boneless
  chicken thighs, cut
  into strips
½ cucumber, thinly sliced
1 sliced shallot
rice vinegar, to taste

For the marinade

1 garlic clove, crushed
small piece of fresh root
  ginger, finely grated
1 lemongrass stalk,
  chopped
2 tsp curry powder
½ tsp turmeric
1 tbsp soy sauce
1 tbsp fish sauce
4 tbsp coconut milk

For the peanut sauce

2 tbsp crunchy peanut
  butter
5 tbsp coconut milk
2 tsp soy sauce
2 tsp fish sauce
1 tbsp lime juice
Asian hot chilli sauce,
  to taste

These chicken skewers are great on their own with the cucumber salad, or as a starter wrapped in DIY lettuce bowls. Freeze the leftover coconut milk to use another time.

Soak 8 wooden skewers in water for 10 minutes, or use metal ones. Mix the marinade ingredients in a bowl, add the chicken strips and toss to coat them. Leave to marinate for 15 minutes.

To make the sauce, put all the ingredients in a small saucepan, add enough boiling water to make a dippable sauce and heat. Add chilli sauce to give it as much heat as you like.

Thread the marinated chicken onto the metal or soaked wooden skewers. Heat a griddle pan or the grill to hot, then grill the chicken skewers, turning them frequently, until they're golden and cooked all the way through.

Toss the cucumber and shallot with a little vinegar in a bowl and serve this alongside the chicken and peanut sauce.

Per serving 462 kcals, **protein** 43.5g, **carbohydrate** 10.1g, **fat** 27.7g, **saturated fat** 14.9g, **fibre** 3.6g, **salt** 5.7g

Chicken Parmigiana light

40 minutes | serves 4 | easy

3 slices of ciabatta
  (about 50g)
olive oil
1 garlic clove, sliced
pinch of chilli flakes
400g can of chopped
  tomatoes
handful of basil leaves,
  chopped, plus extra torn
  leaves, to serve
4 skinless chicken breasts
1 ball of mozzarella, sliced
salt and freshly ground
  black pepper

What makes this chicken Parmigiana light is that the chicken breasts are butterflied and not breaded. However, topped with mozzarella and a few golden crumbs of ciabatta, you won't feel like you are missing out.

Preheat the oven to 200°C/Fan 180°C/Gas 6. Tear the ciabatta into a mix of chunky pieces and smaller crumbs then toss them with a little olive oil and season. Spread the torn ciabatta on a baking tray and cook for 5–10 minutes, until golden. Remove from the oven and set aside.

Heat 1 tablespoon of olive oil in a pan. Add the garlic and cook for a minute, then add the chilli flakes and stir. Tip in the tomatoes and a splash of water if the mixture is very thick, then simmer for 10 minutes. Stir in the chopped basil and remove from the heat.

Butterfly the chicken breasts (cut them horizontally through the thick part of the breast and open them up like a book). Put the butterflied breasts between two pieces of cling film and bash them out with a meat hammer or rolling pin to an even thickness. Heat a little oil in a frying pan, season the chicken and fry the breasts for 3 minutes on each side, then put them on a baking tray. Spoon some tomato sauce on each, then top with the mozzarella slices. Bake in the oven for 10 minutes, or until the cheese has melted. Scatter over the ciabatta crumbs and some fresh, torn basil, and serve.

Per serving 299 kcals, **protein** 38.2g, **carbohydrate** 9.3g, **fat** 11.8g, **saturated fat** 5.2g, **fibre** 1.4g, **salt** 0.8g

Chicken with agrodolce sauce

20 minutes | serves 2 | easy

2 skinless chicken breasts
1 tbsp plain flour, well
  seasoned
1 tbsp olive oil
1 red onion, halved and
  thinly sliced
3 celery sticks, trimmed
  and thinly sliced
100g cherry tomatoes,
  halved
1 tbsp red wine vinegar
½ tsp sugar
small handful of flat-leaf
  parsley, leaves chopped
salt and freshly ground
  black pepper
watercress or rocket,
  to serve

Agrodolce means sweet and sour in Italian. This dish cooks thin escalopes of chicken in a tomato, onion and red wine vinegar sauce for a punchy super-low-cal and low-fat dish.

Slice the chicken breasts in half horizontally so that you have four thin pieces. Cover them with baking paper and flatten them gently with a rolling pin or the base of a heavy pan. Remove the baking paper and dust the chicken breasts with the seasoned flour, shaking off any excess.

Heat the olive oil in a non-stick frying pan and brown the chicken pieces well on both sides. Remove them from the heat and set aside. Cook the onion and celery in the same pan for 3 minutes and season. Add the tomatoes and cook for 3–4 minutes until they start to break down, then add the vinegar and sugar. Put the chicken back in the pan and cook for 3–4 minutes until cooked through, then stir in the parsley. Serve the chicken and agrodolce sauce with watercress or rocket.

Per serving 262 kcals, **protein** 35.8g, **carbohydrate** 13.5g, **fat** 7.6g, **saturated fat** 1.3g, **fibre** 2.3g, **salt** 1.59g

Tamarind chicken with tomato and mint salad

30 minutes | serves 4 | easy

4 skinless chicken breasts, cut into bite-sized pieces
3 tbsp tamarind purée
small piece of fresh root ginger, peeled and grated
3 tsp mild chilli powder
pinch of golden caster sugar
250g cherry tomatoes, halved
½ small red onion, sliced
handful of mint leaves, chopped
1 green chilli, deseeded and sliced
1 lemon, ½ juiced, ½ cut into wedges or 'cheeks', to serve
salt and freshly ground black pepper

Taramind gives these little skewers a nice kick. You can find taramind purée in the spice aisle of your local supermarket.

Soak 12 wooden skewers in water for 10 minutes, or use metal ones. Put the chunks of chicken in a bowl with the tamarind purée, grated ginger and 2 teaspoons of the chilli powder. Add the sugar, season, then toss everything together well and leave to marinate for 10 minutes. Preheat the grill to high.

Meanwhile, mix the tomatoes, onion, mint leaves, green chilli, the remaining chilli powder and the lemon juice together in a bowl. Season and mix again. Thread the marinated meat onto the skewers and grill for about 8 minutes, turning, until golden and cooked through. Serve with the tomato and mint salad, and the lemon for squeezing.

Per serving 195 kcals, **protein** 36g, **carbohydrate** 7.7g, **fat** 2.4g, **saturated fat** 0.7g, **fibre** 1g, **salt** 1.27g

Chicken and ham pie

1 hour 15 minutes | serves 6 | easy

25g butter
1 medium shallot, finely
    chopped
1 garlic clove, crushed
25g plain flour
200ml chicken stock
100ml white wine
4 tbsp single cream
mild olive oil spray
4 large sheets of filo pastry
    (about 125g)
200g thick-sliced lean
    smoked ham, cut into
    bite-sized chunks
400g cooked skinless
    chicken or turkey breast,
    cut into bite-sized
    chunks
salt and freshly ground
    black pepper

Made with crunchy filo pastry rather than puff, this is a healthy alternative to your usual chicken pie.

Preheat the oven to 220°C/Fan 200°C/Gas 7. Melt the butter in a saucepan and cook the shallot and garlic until soft. Stir in the flour, cook briefly, then add the stock and wine. Simmer for 3 minutes, stirring until thick and whisking out any lumps. Remove the pan from the heat and stir in the cream.

Put a 23cm round springform tin on a baking tray and spray with oil. Place a sheet of filo into the tin, pressing it onto the base and sides. Leave the excess to overhang. Spray with oil and then add a second sheet at an angle to the first. Continue until all the sheets are lining the tin.

Stir the meat into the sauce and season. Spoon the meat sauce into the tin and cover the filling with the overhanging pastry. Spray the pastry with oil and bake for 25 minutes. Serve with a large, lightly dressed salad.

Per serving 268 kcals, **protein** 28.8g, **carbohydrate** 15.5g, **fat** 10g, **saturated fat** 4.7g, **fibre** 0.6g, **salt** 1.59g

Chicken with a mustard crust

25 minutes | serves 4 | easy

1 tbsp Dijon mustard
2 tbsp fresh or dried
   breadcrumbs
1 shallot, finely chopped
1 tbsp butter, softened
grated zest of 1 lemon,
   and the lemon cut
   into wedges
handful of flat-leaf parsley,
   leaves chopped
4 large or 8 small boneless
   chicken thighs, skin
   removed
olive oil, for frying
splash of white wine
   (optional)
250g fettuccine
salt and freshly ground
   black pepper

This makes for a very quick but substantial dish when served with pasta. If you are avoiding carbs, you can serve the chicken with lots of veggies instead.

Mix the mustard with the breadcrumbs, shallot, butter, lemon zest and parsley in a bowl, season, then spread the mixture onto the chicken thighs.

Heat a splash of olive oil in an ovenproof lidded frying pan and put the thighs in the pan crust-side up. Fry for 5 minutes, then add a splash of wine or water, cover, and cook for a further 5 minutes. Meanwhile, cook the fettuccine according to the packet instructions and preheat the grill to high.

Take the lid off the pan and put it under the grill for 5 minutes, or until the crust on the chicken is browned and bubbling and the chicken is cooked through. Serve with the fettuccine, lemon wedges and any juices from the pan.

Per serving 451 kcals, **protein** 34g, **carbohydrate** 51.5g, **fat** 13.5g, **saturated fat** 4.2g, **fibre** 1.8g, **salt** 0.74g

Tarragon chicken

45 minutes | serves 4 | easy

1 tbsp sunflower oil
2 shallots, sliced
2 garlic cloves, crushed
8 boneless, skinless
  chicken thighs, trimmed
  of all fat
100ml dry white wine
400ml chicken stock
½ tbsp cornflour
½ tbsp cold water
3 tbsp half-fat crème
  fraîche
2 tbsp roughly snipped
  tarragon leaves
salt and freshly ground
  black pepper

A quick, light but creamy dish that will be sure to satisfy. Serve with new potatoes and green beans.

Heat the oil in a large non-stick frying pan and fry the shallots gently for 5 minutes, until soft and lightly coloured. Add the garlic for the last minute of the cooking time.

Season the chicken thighs and add them to the pan. Fry for 2–3 minutes, turning them over once, until very lightly coloured. Pour in the wine and bring to the boil. Stir in the stock and simmer gently for 10 minutes.

Mix the cornflour and water together then stir them into the pan. As soon as the sauce thickens, stir in the crème fraîche and tarragon, then season. Remove the pan from the heat and serve with new potatoes and green beans if you like.

Per serving 295 kcals, **protein** 39.6g, **carbohydrate** 5.1g, **fat** 11.1g, **saturated fat** 4.1g, **fibre** 0.7g, **salt** 0.07g

Chicken, leek and Dijon mustard casserole

45 minutes | serves 2 | easy

olive oil, for frying

4 whole skin-on chicken thighs

1 leek, washed and finely chopped

2 tsp Dijon mustard

250ml chicken stock

210g can of butter beans, drained and rinsed

salt and freshly ground black pepper

handful of flat-leaf parsley, chopped, to serve

An easy, healthy casserole is hard to come by, but this dish ticks both the boxes, and it's delicious to boot. Serve with a small side of rice or a lightly dressed salad.

Heat a little oil in a large, deep lidded pan and fry the chicken all over until browned (but not cooked through). Remove the chicken and set aside, then add the leek and fry until softened. Stir in the mustard and stock and bring to a simmer. Tip in the butter beans, season and stir.

Sit the chicken thighs skin-side up on top of the bean and leek mixture. Cover and simmer for 25–30 minutes. Scatter over the parsley and serve.

Per serving 385 kcals, **protein** 35.8g, **carbohydrate** 9.1g, **fat** 22.7g, **saturated fat** 6g, **fibre** 4.4g, **salt** 1.6g

One-pot chicken with cannellini beans and chorizo

1 hour | serves 2 | easy

olive oil, for greasing
4 whole skin-on chicken
  thighs
1 red onion, cut into thin
  wedges
100ml light chicken stock
  or water
5cm chunk of hot chorizo,
  cut into small dice
400g can of cannellini
  beans, drained and
  rinsed
½ tsp rosemary leaves,
  chopped, plus extra
  to garnish
salt and freshly ground
  black pepper

This one-pot chicken dish requires minimal hands-on time. What's more, it comes in at under 300 calories, making it very diet-friendly indeed.

Preheat the oven to 200°C/Fan 180°C/Gas 6 and grease a baking dish or roasting tin. Put the chicken thighs skin-side up in the dish or tin, and tuck the onion underneath the thighs.

Season generously, then pour the chicken stock or water in the pan. Roast for 30 minutes, then add the chorizo and cook for another 15 minutes. Tip in the beans and rosemary and stir everything together (including the onion). Roast for another 10 minutes, sprinkle with some rosemary leaves and serve.

Per serving 247 kcals, **protein** 32.5g, **carbohydrate** 10.5g, **fat** 7.4g, **saturated fat** 2.4g, **fibre** 4.5g, **salt** 0.5g

Sherry-braised chicken breast with horseradish crumbs

30 minutes | serves 2 | easy

large handful of chunky
  breadcrumbs
1 tbsp grated horseradish
  from a jar, drained
2 tsp olive oil
2 small skinless chicken
  breasts
2 tsp plain flour, well
  seasoned
1 red onion, thinly sliced
1 garlic clove, thinly sliced
150ml sherry
salt and freshly ground
  black pepper
100g tenderstem broccoli,
  steamed, to serve

Sherry and chicken make the perfect pair. Serve with tenderstem broccoli or, if you aren't watching your waistline, accompany with roast potatoes.

Preheat the oven to 200°C/Fan 180°C/Gas 6. Spread the breadcrumbs on a baking sheet, add the horseradish to the crumbs along with 1 teaspoon of the olive oil and season. Mix well and toast in the oven for 8–10 minutes, until golden. Remove from the oven and set aside.

Dust the chicken in the seasoned flour. Heat the remaining olive oil in a frying pan and fry the chicken on both sides until golden. Remove the chicken and set aside then, in the same pan, fry the onion and garlic until soft. Pour in the sherry and put the chicken back in the pan. Let it cook for a further 5–7 minutes, or until the chicken is cooked through. Serve with the breadcrumbs sprinkled over the top and some tenderstem broccoli.

Per serving 285 kcals, **protein** 32.5g, **carbohydrate** 18g, **fat** 5.8g, **saturated fat** 1.1g, **fibre** 1.5g, **salt** 0.41g

Roast chicken with 40 cloves of garlic

1 hour 40 minutes, plus resting | serves 6 | easy

1 whole chicken
 (about 1.5kg)
olive oil
3 sprigs of thyme
1 lemon, sliced
4 garlic bulbs, cloves
 separated, skin left on
glass of white wine or
 water
salt and freshly ground
 black pepper

Roasting the chicken with garlic and wine makes the dish creamy, soft and mellow. Serve with a lightly dressed salad or lots of vegetables to make a perfect healthy meal, packed with flavour.

Preheat the oven to 200°C/Fan 180°C/Gas 6. Rub the chicken all over with oil and season generously inside and out. Put the thyme and half the lemon slices inside the bird with a few garlic cloves. Put the remaining garlic and lemon slices in an ovenproof baking dish with the wine or water.

Sit the chicken on top of the garlic and lemon and roast for 1½ hours, until golden and cooked through. Cover loosely with foil and rest for 20 minutes then serve the chicken with the garlic and strained roasting juices.

Per serving 371 kcals, **protein** 32.4g, **carbohydrate** 3.8g, **fat** 24.5g, **saturated fat** 6.9g, **fibre** 0.7g, **salt** 0.29g

Quick and easy

Chicken, pea and pasta broth

15 minutes | serves 2 | easy

750ml chicken stock
50g tiny pasta shapes
  (or rice)
1 skinless cooked chicken
  breast, shredded
50g frozen peas, defrosted
small handful of flat-leaf
  parsley, leaves chopped
salt and freshly ground
  black pepper

Chicken, pea and pasta broth is one of our go-to comfort food recipes. A low-fat family favourite that always pleases, it's also ready in under 20 minutes.

Heat the chicken stock in a pan, add the pasta and cook for about 8 minutes, until just tender. Add the chicken and peas and cook for 1 minute until heated through. Season, then stir through the parsley and serve.

Per serving 290 kcals, **protein** 37.2g, **carbohydrate** 24g, **fat** 5.9g, **saturated fat** 0.9g, **fibre** 2.9g, **salt** 2.01g

Chicken broth with orecchiette, pancetta and peas

20 minutes | serves 2 | easy

olive oil, for frying
2 shallots, finely chopped
70g diced pancetta
750ml chicken stock
50g orecchiette
50g frozen peas
Parmesan cheese, grated,
   to serve (optional)
salt and freshly ground
   black pepper
crusty bread, to serve

This soup is warming but also light enough to eat in the summer. Orecchiette is a small ear-shaped pasta that works well in soups.

Heat a little olive oil in a large frying pan, add the shallots and pancetta and cook until the shallots have softened. Add the chicken stock and pasta, and cook for 8–10 minutes, or until the pasta is tender. Add the peas and cook for 2–3 minutes. Serve in bowls with grated Parmesan cheese, if using, salt and lots of freshly ground black pepper, and some crusty bread on the side.

Per serving 291 kcals, **protein** 22.5g, **carbohydrate** 21.1g, **fat** 12.9g, **saturated fat** 5.1g, **fibre** 4.2g, **salt** 2g

One-pot chicken with orzo and dill

30 minutes | serves 2 | easy

4 boneless, skinless
  chicken thighs
500ml chicken stock
150g orzo
½ small bunch of dill,
  chopped
25g butter
grated zest and juice of
  ½ lemon, and wedges
  of 1 lemon, to serve
salt and freshly ground
  black pepper

Another healthy way with pasta. This easy recipe pairs grain-shaped orzo pasta with chicken and fragrant dill. Ready to plate in under 30 minutes, this is perfect as a speedy lunch or mid-week meal.

Put the chicken thighs and stock in a wide, shallow pan. Bring to a simmer then cook for 10 minutes. Add the orzo, cover and cook for another 6–8 minutes, or until the pasta is tender and the chicken is cooked through.

Remove the thighs from the stock, set aside until they're cool enough to handle, then shred the meat. Return the meat to the pan with the dill, butter, lemon zest and juice. Season and serve with lemon wedges on the side.

Per serving 569 kcals, **protein** 52g, **carbohydrate** 53.5g, **fat** 16.3g, **saturated fat** 8.3g, **fibre** 4.2g, **salt** 1.2g

Smoky chicken, sweetcorn and pancetta salad

20 minutes | serves 2 | easy

70g diced pancetta

2 skinless chicken breasts, cut into thin strips

2 sweetcorn cobs, husk and silk removed

extra-virgin olive oil, for greasing and dressing

2 tsp wholegrain mustard

1 tsp runny honey

½ tsp hot smoked paprika

1 small garlic clove, crushed

1 tbsp red wine vinegar

1 tbsp water

2–3 Little Gem lettuce heads, leaves separated

salt and freshly ground black pepper

This salad has a true Tex-Mex feel to it. Top with slices of ripe avocado, if you like.

Heat a non-stick frying pan and add the pancetta. Fry until the fat starts to melt, then add the chicken. Season with pepper, turn up the heat, and fry for 5 minutes, stirring often, until both the pancetta and chicken are golden and cooked through. Remove from the heat and set aside.

Heat a griddle pan or heavy frying pan. Rub the corn with a drop of oil, season, then griddle for 5–8 minutes, turning often, until tender and blackened in places. Meanwhile, whisk 1 tablespoon of oil, the mustard, honey, paprika, garlic and vinegar with the water in a bowl to make a dressing, then season to taste.

Cut the kernels from the griddled corn cobs then toss them with the chicken, pancetta, lettuce and dressing.

Per serving 459 kcals, **protein** 45.6g, **carbohydrate** 21.3g, **fat** 21.8g, **saturated fat** 5.3g, **fibre** 2.4g, **salt** 2.21g

Throw-it-together chicken salad

10 minutes | serves 2 | easy

200g cooked, shredded
  chicken
1 shallot, finely sliced
8 cherry tomatoes, halved
handful of fresh mint
  leaves, chopped
handful of Thai basil leaves,
  chopped

For the dressing
1 garlic clove, crushed
1–2 bird's eye chillies,
  finely chopped
  (deseeded if you like)
4cm piece of fresh root
  ginger, peeled and finely
  grated
juice of 2 limes
2 tbsp palm sugar or soft
  brown sugar
3 tbsp fish sauce

As the name implies, this salad can be easily thrown together with leftover chicken. The chilli, lime and fish sauce give it a fresh Asian feel too. It is just as delicious with regular fresh basil if you can't find Thai basil leaves.

Put the chicken in a serving bowl with the shallot and cherry tomatoes. Mix the dressing ingredients together and pour over the chicken.

Add the herbs and toss everything together to serve.

Per serving 296 kcals, **protein** 31.4g, **carbohydrate** 24.4g, **fat** 7.8g, **saturated fat** 2.2g, **fibre** 1.2g, **salt** 4.8g

Griddled chicken salad with basil mayo

30 minutes | serves 4 | easy

½ red onion, finely sliced
1 tbsp white wine vinegar
½ sourdough loaf
olive oil, for drizzling and
brushing
30g Parmesan cheese,
grated,
6 boneless, skinless
chicken thigh fillets
4 tbsp mayonnaise
½ small bunch of basil,
leaves shredded
1 romaine lettuce, leaves
separated and torn
salt and freshly ground
black pepper

This griddled chicken salad with basil mayo makes a satisfying lunch or a lighter evening meal. It's full of flavour and is ready in just 30 minutes.

Put the sliced onion in a bowl with the vinegar. Toss and set to one side. Preheat the oven to 180°C/Fan 160°C/Gas 4.

Cut the bread at an angle to make nice long slices. Place the bread on a baking tray, drizzle with olive oil, then bake for 10 minutes, until golden. Scatter the grated Parmesan over the bread slices and bake for another couple of minutes. Remove from the oven and set aside.

Brush the chicken thighs with olive oil and season generously. Heat a griddle pan or heavy frying pan and cook the thighs for about 10–15 minutes, or until golden brown and cooked through. Slice thinly.

Mix the mayonnaise into the onion and vinegar then stir in the basil. Arrange the torn lettuce leaves on a serving platter. Scatter over the sliced, grilled chicken and croutons. Drizzle over the basil mayo (add a splash of water if you need to, to make it runnier).

Per serving 553 kcals, **protein** 43.3g, **carbohydrate** 22.4g, **fat** 32.8g, **saturated fat** 7g, **fibre** 2.1g, **salt** 1.22g

Chargrilled chicken with white beans and cabbage

25 minutes | serves 2 | easy

1 large skinless chicken
  breast
olive oil
grated zest and juice of
  1 lemon
5 spring onions, whites and
  greens separated and
  finely sliced
2 garlic cloves, sliced
250g Savoy cabbage,
  shredded
400g can of cannellini
  beans, drained and
  rinsed
200ml chicken stock
100ml double cream
salt and freshly ground
  black pepper

This is a very quick way to turn one chicken breast into a substantial after-work meal for two.

Butterfly the chicken breast by slicing it in half horizontally to make two thinner pieces. Put the chicken pieces between two sheets of cling film and, using a meat hammer or rolling pin, gently bash them to flatten them out to an even thickness. Transfer the chicken pieces to a shallow bowl. Mix 1 tablespoon of olive oil with 1 tablespoon of the lemon juice, half the lemon zest and some seasoning and rub the mixture all over the chicken. Leave to marinate while you start the beans.

Heat a splash of oil in a frying pan, add the white parts of the spring onions and the garlic and cook gently until soft. Stir in the cabbage and remaining lemon zest, cook for 1 minute, then add the cannellini beans and stock. Simmer for 8–10 minutes, until the cabbage is tender and the stock is almost all gone.

Meanwhile, heat a griddle pan or heavy frying pan until smoking hot, then add the chicken and cook for 2–3 minutes on each side until cooked through and charred.

Stir the remaining lemon juice and the cream into the beans with the green parts of the spring onions and heat through before seasoning. Serve with the chargrilled chicken.

Per serving 549 kcals, **protein** 33.8g, **carbohydrate** 22g, **fat** 36.3g, **saturated fat** 18.4g, **fibre** 14g, **salt** 0.4g

Harissa chicken patties with quinoa salad

30 minutes | serves 4 | easy

250g quinoa

500g lean chicken mince

1–2 tbsp harissa paste (depending how much spice you want)

1 red onion, ½ grated and ½ thinly sliced

olive oil, for frying and drizzling

large handful of mint leaves, chopped

large handful of flat-leaf parsley, chopped

seeds of 1 pomegranate

2 oranges, peeled, segmented, and membrane removed

salt and freshly ground pepper

These healthy, fiery patties transform minced chicken into a Moroccan feast, and the pomegranate seeds in the herby salad add a welcome, refreshing burst of juice.

Cook the quinoa according to the packet instructions. Once cooked, rinse under cold running water and drain thoroughly.

Meanwhile, mix the mince, harissa paste and grated onion in a bowl with some seasoning, until well combined. Roll into small walnut-sized balls. Heat 1 tablespoon of oil in a large non-stick frying pan. Fry the patties for around 15 minutes, turning them until they are golden all over and cooked through.

Mix the quinoa with the sliced onion, mint, parsley, pomegranate seeds, orange segments, a drizzle more olive oil and plenty of salt and pepper. Serve the patties with the quinoa salad and drizzle over the spicy pan juices.

Per serving 444 kcals, **protein** 38.7g, **carbohydrate** 48.3g, **fat** 12g, **saturated fat** 1.7g, **fibre** 3.2g, **salt** 0.34g

Chicken liver, hazelnut, pancetta and apple salad

20 minutes | serves 2 | easy

6 slices of pancetta
250g chicken livers,
  trimmed and patted dry
100g bag of salad leaves
1 eating apple, cored and
  finely sliced
2 tbsp toasted hazelnuts,
  roughly chopped
½ bunch of spring onions,
  thinly sliced
1 tbsp olive oil
2 tsp cider vinegar
1 tbsp water
salt and freshly ground
  black pepper

Chicken liver may not be everyone's cup of tea, but it is low in fat and full of nutrients, and it works beautifully with salty pancetta, crunchy apple and toasted nuts.

Heat a non-stick frying pan and add the pancetta. Cook for 1–2 minutes, until sizzling and crisp. Take the pancetta out of the pan and set aside.

Season the livers, then fry them in the pancetta fat for 2–3 minutes on a high heat, or until well browned and just pink in the middle. Lift them out of the pan, set them aside, and let the pan cool for a few minutes.

Scatter the salad leaves, apple slices, chopped hazelnuts and onions over two plates. Whisk the olive oil, vinegar and water into the pan juices, then season. Top the salad with the livers and crisp pancetta, then spoon over the dressing and serve.

Per serving 343 kcals, **protein** 29.4g, **carbohydrate** 9.5g, **fat** 21g, **saturated fat** 4.2g, **fibre** 2.6g, **salt** 1.32g

Chicken skewers with bulgar wheat and corn salad

30 minutes | serves 2 | easy

100g bulgar wheat
½ tsp celery salt
1 tsp ground coriander
2 skinless chicken breasts,
    cut into chunks
2 sweetcorn cobs, husk
    and silk removed
½ small red onion, cut into
    half moons
6 cherry tomatoes, halved
large handful of basil,
    leaves finely chopped
1 tbsp white wine vinegar
1 tbsp extra-virgin olive oil
salt and freshly ground
    black pepper

A simple spice rub peps up this delicious, quick and easy mid-week meal, and bulgar wheat makes a welcome change from couscous.

Soak 6 wooden skewers in water for 10 minutes, or use metal ones. Put the bulgar wheat in a heat-proof bowl and cover it with boiling water, then cover the bowl with cling film and set aside to soak for 10–15 minutes, or until tender.

Combine the celery salt, coriander and a little freshly ground black pepper. Rub the mix into the chunks of chicken, thread the chicken onto the skewers and set aside. Preheat the grill.

Cook the corn in boiling water for 10 minutes, and then – as soon as they are cool enough to handle – cut the kernels from the cobs. Fluff up the bulgar wheat and add the corn, onion and tomatoes.

Mix the basil, vinegar and oil in a small bowl along with some seasoning.

Cook the chicken skewers under the grill for 3–4 minutes on each side, or until the chicken is cooked through. Serve with the salad, and the dressing drizzled over both.

Per serving 484 kcals, **protein** 43g, **carbohydrate**, 58.7g, **fat** 10.2g, **saturated fat** 1.4g, **fibre** 2.1g, **salt** 1g

Italian chicken and basil burgers with tomato relish

25 minutes | serves 4 | easy

2 tbsp cider vinegar
1 tsp golden caster sugar
½ tsp yellow mustard seeds
500g lean chicken or
  turkey mince
small bunch of basil,
  leaves torn
1 egg yolk
1 tbsp olive oil
2 tomatoes, chopped
4 spring onions, sliced
4 bread buns, split and
  toasted
1 ball of mozzarella, torn
  into pieces
salt and freshly ground
  black pepper

**This Italian twist on your classic chicken burger is light and fragrant.
Serve alongside a fresh green salad or skinny fries.**

Heat the vinegar, sugar and mustard seeds in a small saucepan, until
the sugar dissolves. Bring to the boil and simmer for 1 minute, then
leave to cool.

Mix the mince, torn basil leaves and egg yolk with lots of seasoning.
Form into 4 burgers. Heat the oil in a frying pan and cook the burgers
for 7 minutes on each side, or until golden and cooked through.

Stir the tomatoes and spring onions into the cider vinegar dressing.
Serve the burgers in the toasted buns, topped with torn mozzarella and
the tomato relish.

Per serving 532 kcals, **protein** 52g, **carbohydrate** 42.5g, **fat** 17g, **saturated fat** 6.7g, **fibre** 2.6g, **salt** 1.5g

Chicken and slaw baguette with hazelnut dressing

30 minutes | serves 4 | easy

½ large or 1 whole small
  summer cabbage
1 large or 2 small carrots
4 radishes
juice of 1 lime
1 tbsp sweet chilli sauce,
  or sriracha if you like a
  hit of chilli
2 tbsp olive oil, plus extra
  for frying
2 tbsp chopped coriander
60g hazelnuts, finely
  chopped (blanched or
  skin on)
2 skinless, boneless
  chicken breasts, halved
  horizontally
1–2 baguettes
salt and freshly ground
  black pepper
mayonnaise, to serve

These sandwiches are great for picnics or lunch, and are a fabulous way to use up any leftover chicken from your Sunday roast. You can use any type of cabbage you like but summer red cabbage is ideal as it give this dish lots of colour.

Finely shred the cabbage and tip it into a large bowl. Finely shred or grate the carrot(s) and add it to the cabbage. Finely slice the radishes and add these to the bowl too. Mix the lime juice and chilli sauce or sriracha in a small bowl with the olive oil and coriander. Tip the dressing over the cabbage mix, add the hazelnuts and toss everything together well.

Heat a little oil in a frying pan, season the halved chicken breasts and fry them on both sides until they are browned a little at the edges and cooked through. Transfer the chicken pieces to a board and slice them into strips.

Cut the baguette(s) into sections and cut them open down the centre like a book. Spread with mayonnaise, stuff with the slaw and chicken and add more chilli if you like. These baguettes will keep well for a few hours, wrapped, so are ideal for taking on a picnic, but as they contain chicken you must keep them cold.

Per serving 549 kcals, **protein** 26.7g, **carbohydrate** 65.6g, **fat** 19.1g, **saturated fat** 2.2g, **fibre** 9g, **salt** 1.3g

Coconut chicken and rice one-pot

30 minutes | serves 4 | easy

400ml can of half-fat
  coconut milk
200ml chicken stock
3cm piece of fresh root
  ginger, peeled and thinly
  sliced
1 lemongrass stalk, woody
  outer leaves removed
  and tender stalk finely
  chopped
6 skinless chicken thigh
  fillets, quartered
250g basmati rice
½ bunch of spring onions,
  shredded
2 green chillies, shredded
  (deseeded if you like)
½ bunch of coriander,
  chopped
salt and freshly ground
  black pepper

This is pure Asian comfort food, and it's incredibly easy to make, as it needs no initial frying of the ingredients. It also requires very little washing up!

Put the coconut milk, chicken stock, ginger and lemongrass in a wide shallow pan with a lid. Bring to a simmer, then cover and cook for 5 minutes.

Remove the lid, add the chicken and rice. Stir, then bring back to a simmer. Reduce the heat to the lowest setting, cover then leave for 15–20 minutes until the stock is absorbed and the rice is tender. Fluff up the rice, season, then scatter over the spring onions, chillies and coriander to serve.

Per serving 496 kcals, **protein** 27.5g, **carbohydrate** 48g, **fat** 19.6g, **saturated fat** 7.4g, **fibre** 0.6g, **salt** 0.3g

Mango chicken with couscous

15 minutes | serves 2 | easy

1 tbsp olive oil

about 350g mini chicken
fillets, or 2 skinless
chicken breasts, cut into
thin strips

2 tsp ground cumin

300ml hot chicken stock

150g couscous

3 tbsp mango chutney

4 spring onions, sliced into
3cm pieces

small handful of coriander,
leaves roughly chopped

**Beautifully flavoured, this dish will be ready for the table in just
15 minutes – perfect for busy days.**

Heat the oil in a wok or large frying pan. Sprinkle the chicken fillets or strips
with the ground cumin and fry for a couple of minutes, until lightly browned.

Put the couscous in a heatproof bowl and pour over 200ml of the chicken
stock. Cover and leave to soak for 5 minutes.

Add the mango chutney to the chicken, stir well and leave to simmer for
2 minutes, then add the remaining chicken stock and the spring onions
and simmer for 5 minutes, or until the chicken is cooked through. Fluff
up the couscous with a fork, stir half the coriander through the couscous
and the remainder through the chicken, then serve.

Per serving 505 kcals, **protein** 53.6g, **carbohydrate** 52.6g, **fat** 10.4g, **saturated fat** 1.5g, **fibre** 0.5g, **salt** 1.8g

Tagliatelle with roast chicken

20 minutes | serves 2 | easy

150g tagliatelle or thin
  pappardelle
200g roast chicken, cut
  into bite-sized pieces
  (and any leftover
  roasting juices)
small handful of fresh soft
  herbs such as tarragon,
  basil or parsley (1 herb or
  a combination of herbs),
  roughly chopped
salt and freshly ground
  black pepper

This is a good way to use up leftover roast chicken and it's very easy to make. Retaining the juices from the chicken roasting tin and tossing them through the cooked pasta adds bags of flavour, so be sure not to throw them away.

Cook the pasta in plenty of boiling, salted water according to the packet instructions, then drain.

Put the leftover chicken roasting juices (strained if necessary) into a saucepan over a low heat, then add the chicken pieces and reheat them in the juices. Put the drained tagliatelle into a big bowl and add the warm chicken and some seasoning. Add the herbs, then toss with enough roasting juices to coat the pasta and serve.

Per serving 386 kcals, **protein** 35.6g, **carbohydrate** 39.8g, **fat** 9.3g, **saturated fat** 2.1g, **fibre** 0.2g, **salt** 0.3g

Chicken with green olives, rosemary and tomatoes

35 minutes | serves 4 | easy

1 tsp olive oil
6 chicken thigh fillets, trimmed of all fat and halved
2 garlic cloves, sliced
2 rosemary sprigs, leaves stripped and chopped
2 x 400g tins of chopped tomatoes
400g tin of cannellini beans, drained and rinsed
10 green olives, pitted and halved
salt and freshly ground black pepper
crusty bread, to serve

This one-pan chicken stew is incredibly easy to make and requires minimal washing up. Serve with crusty bread to dip in the tomatoey sauce.

Heat the oil in a large non-stick frying pan. Fry the chicken over a fairly high heat until golden.

Remove the chicken from the pan and add the garlic and rosemary. Cook for 1 minute, then add the tomatoes and bring to a simmer. Add the chicken and cook for 20 minutes, until the sauce has thickened. Stir in the beans and olives. Season and cook for another 10 minutes and serve with crusty bread and a large salad if you like.

Per serving 258 kcals, **protein** 34.2g, **carbohydrate** 16.6g, **fat** 6.5g, **saturated fat** 1.7g, **fibre** 5.7g, **salt** 1.44g

Chicken stuffed with spinach and dates

30 minutes | serves 4 | easy

olive oil

1 large onion, thinly sliced

2 garlic cloves, sliced

4 ready-to-eat pitted dates, finely chopped

200g spinach, chopped

2 tsp ground cumin

4 skinless chicken breasts

2 tbsp pomegranate molasses or honey

salt and freshly ground black pepper

steamed green beans, to serve

Dates make this dish sweet and full of flavour. Serve with steamed green beans for a quick, healthy meal.

Preheat the oven to 200°C/Fan 180°C/Gas 6. Heat a little olive oil in a non-stick frying pan and cook the onion and garlic with some seasoning for 5 minutes, then add the dates, spinach and half the ground cumin. Cook for a further 1–2 minutes, then remove from the heat.

Cut the chicken breasts lengthways so they open like a book. Divide the stuffing between the breasts, fold to close and put the breasts in a shallow baking dish. Rub the remaining cumin over the chicken and season. Drizzle over the pomegranate molasses or honey then bake for 20 minutes. Remove from the oven and serve with green beans.

Per serving 252 kcals, protein 36.4g, carbohydrate 17.7g, fat 4.4g, saturated fat 0.9g, fibre 2.2g, salt 0.41g

Chicken, pancetta and mushroom stew

30 minutes | serves 4 | easy

15g dried porcini
  mushrooms
200ml boiling water
100g diced pancetta or
  bacon
500g skinless chicken thigh
  fillets, quartered
1 onion, chopped
2 garlic cloves, chopped
5 tbsp balsamic vinegar
150ml red wine
1 tbsp cornflour, dissolved
  in 1 tbsp cold water
salt and freshly ground
  black pepper
mashed potatoes or
  pappardelle, to serve
handful of flat-leaf parsley,
  chopped, to serve

This low-calorie stew is very easy to make. Chicken thighs are more flavoursome and tender than breasts, but you can use breast meat if you prefer. If you serve with pappardelle or mash, be aware they will add extra calories!

Place the dried porcini in a heatproof bowl, and pour over the boiling water. Set to one side for 10 minutes, then strain and reserve 125ml of the soaking liquid. Rinse the mushrooms to remove any grit, then chop.

Heat a frying pan and fry the pancetta or bacon until crisp. Scoop it out with a slotted spoon and leave to drain on kitchen paper. Season and fry the chicken in the oil left by the pancetta on both sides until cooked through, then remove.

Add the onion, chopped porcini and garlic to the pan with some salt and cook for about 4 minutes, until softened. Add the vinegar and increase the heat. Let it sizzle for 1 minute then stir in the porcini soaking liquid, red wine, chicken and cornflour liquid. Cook, uncovered, for 20 minutes.

Serve with mashed potatoes or pappardelle pasta, lots of freshly ground black pepper and flat-leaf parsley sprinkled over the top.

Per serving 274 kcals, **protein** 33.1g, **carbohydrate** 9.7g, **fat** 10.3g, **saturated fat** 3.9g, **fibre** 1.7g, **salt** 1.58g

Paprika chicken with kale and beans

30 minutes | serves 2 | easy

1 tbsp olive oil

1 large onion, halved and thinly sliced

2 garlic cloves, crushed

1 skinless chicken breast, cut into small pieces

1 tsp smoked paprika

250ml dry sherry

400g can of plum tomatoes

400g can of borlotti or cannellini beans, drained and rinsed

100g kale, tough stalks removed and leaves chopped

salt and freshly ground black pepper

A delicious way to get your superfood hit. There is no harm in adding more kale, to ramp up the health factor.

Heat the olive oil in a large frying pan. Add the onion and garlic and season. Cook for 10 minutes, until golden, and then add the chicken. Cook for about 3 minutes, until the chicken is opaque. Add the paprika, sherry, tomatoes and beans.

Cook for 10 minutes, then add the kale and cook for a further 10 minutes. Season with salt and freshly ground black pepper and serve.

Per serving 414 kcals, **protein** 31.3g, **carbohydrate** 37.6g, **fat** 8.8g, **saturated fat** 1.1g, **fibre** 10g, **salt** 0.41g

Chicken, red onion and mushroom stew with sherry and butterbeans

30 minutes | serves 4 | easy

olive oil, for frying
6 skinless chicken thigh
   fillets, quartered
1 tbsp smoked paprika
1 garlic clove, chopped
2 red onions, cut into thick
   wedges
200g chestnut mushrooms,
   thickly sliced
100ml sherry
400ml chicken stock
400g can of chopped
   tomatoes
400g can of butterbeans,
   drained and rinsed
small bunch of flat-leaf
   parsley, roughly chopped,
   to serve
crusty bread, to serve
salt and freshly ground
   black pepper

A satisfying, filling stew with bags of flavour. Perfect for throwing together for a speedy mid-week meal.

Heat a little oil in a frying pan, then add the chicken and fry until golden on all sides. Add the paprika, garlic, onions and mushrooms and cook for about 5 minutes until the mushrooms and onions have softened. Add the remaining ingredients, except the parsley and bread, and bring to the boil.

Turn the heat down to a simmer and cook for a further 15 minutes, season as you like. Serve with a sprinkling of parsley and plenty of crusty bread to mop up the sauce.

Per serving 248 kcals, **protein** 27g, **carbohydrate** 17g, **fat** 5g, **saturated fat** 1g, **fibre** 6g, **salt** 1.2g

Mid-week suppers

Roast lemon chicken with three-grain tabbouleh

1 hour | serves 4 | easy

4 chicken legs
2 tsp olive oil for the
  chicken, plus 3 tbsp
2 lemons
150g rice, spelt and
  barley mix
large bunch of flat-leaf
  parsley, leaves chopped
large bunch of mint, leaves
  chopped
2 shallots, finely chopped
2 tomatoes, diced
salt and freshly ground
  black pepper

Tabbouleh gives this dish a light, fresh feel. You can find a mixed packet of rice, spelt and barley in some supermarkets – it makes a lovely nutty salad base. Alternatively, just use spelt or barley on their own.

Preheat the oven to 200°C/Fan 180°C/Gas 6. Rub the chicken legs with 2 teaspoons of olive oil and season generously. Cut one of the lemons into thick slices and put the slices in the bottom of a baking dish. Sit the chicken legs on top and roast for 45 minutes, until golden and cooked through.

Cook the three-grain mix according to the packet instructions, until tender. Drain, then rinse under cold running water and drain again. Tip into a large bowl and add the parsley, mint, shallots and tomatoes, the juice of the remaining lemon and the remaining olive oil. Season and toss together. Carve the chicken in two between the drumstick and the thigh, and serve on top of the tabbouleh.

Per serving 573 kcals, **protein** 28.3g, **carbohydrate** 30.2g, **fat** 38.5g, **saturated fat** 9.1g, **fibre** 2.3g, **salt** 0.31g

Moroccan chicken and herb salad

40 minutes | serves 2 | easy

1 medium courgette, sliced

1 small red onion, cut into
8 wedges

1 yellow pepper, deseeded
and cut into small chunks

olive oil spray

2 skinless chicken breasts
(each about 150g)

1 tbsp harissa paste

100g bulgar wheat, rinsed
under cold running water
and drained thoroughly

small bunch of coriander,
leaves roughly chopped

small bunch of mint, leaves
roughly chopped

2 tbsp low-fat natural
yoghurt

salt and freshly ground
black pepper

2 lemon wedges, to serve

This makes an easy, flavourful supper. You can also double the serving size and take any leftovers with you for lunch the following day.

Preheat the oven to 200°C/Fan 180°C/Gas 6. Put the vegetables on a baking tray and spritz with oil. Season and roast for 15 minutes.

Slash each chicken breast four times and rub over the harissa.

Take the roasted vegetables out of the oven and turn them over. Add the chicken to the tray and cook for 18–20 minutes until cooked through. Leave to cool. Meanwhile, cook the bulgar wheat according to the packet instructions.

Transfer the vegetables and any cooking juices to a large bowl and add the cooked bulgar wheat. Add the herbs, season, and toss.

Put the salad in two shallow bowls or deep containers. Slice the chicken and sit it on top of each serving. Spoon over the yoghurt and add lemon wedges to serve.

Per serving 425 kcals, protein 46.3g, carbohydrate 46.6g, fat 5.1g, saturated fat 1g, fibre 2.4g, salt 0.4g

Chicken and almond pilaf

40 minutes | serves 2 | easy

50g butter
4 skinless chicken thigh
   fillets, cut into bite-sized
   pieces
1 onion, halved and sliced
6 cardamom pods, split
   and seeds crushed
150g basmati rice, rinsed
300ml chicken stock
2 tbsp chopped dill
handful of flaked almonds,
   toasted
salt and freshly ground
   black pepper
lemon wedges, to serve

Serve this one-pot pilaf as a main for two or as a side for four, with lots of leafy greens.

Melt half the butter in a saucepan with a lid, season the chicken then cook all over until browned. Remove the chicken and set to one side, then add the onion and the remaining butter and cook until soft and golden.

Return the chicken to the pan with the crushed cardamom seeds and stir well. Tip in the rice, stir, then add the chicken stock.

Bring to the boil, turn down to a simmer, cover and cook over a very low heat for 12–15 minutes, until all the stock has been absorbed and the rice is tender (you might need to add a little more stock). Season then stir in the dill, scatter over the almonds to finish, and serve with lemon wedges.

Per serving 744 kcals, **protein** 48.9g, **carbohydrate** 67.3g, **fat** 32.9g, **saturated fat** 15.5g, **fibre** 2.8g, **salt** 2.04g

Yoghurt-spiced chicken with almond and coriander rice

30 minutes | serves 2 | easy

150g natural yoghurt

1 tbsp madras or other
 Indian curry paste

2 skinless chicken breasts

knob of butter

1 onion, halved and sliced

3 cardamom pods, lightly
 crushed

150g brown basmati rice,
 rinsed

350ml chicken stock

1 tbsp flaked almonds,
 toasted

1 red chilli, finely chopped
 (optional or deseeded if
 you like)

½ bunch of coriander,
 leaves chopped

This super-speedy spiced yoghurt marinade doesn't need hours to work its magic – in 30 minutes dinner is served.

Mix the yoghurt and curry paste and toss with the chicken breasts. Melt the butter in a wide, shallow pan with a lid. Add the onion and cardamom pods and fry for 5 minutes, then tip in the rice and stock. Bring it all to a simmer, cover and cook until all the stock is absorbed and the rice is tender (you might need to add a little more stock).

Heat a griddle or grill and cook the chicken breasts until golden and cooked through. Stir the almonds, chilli (if using) and coriander through the rice. Slice the breasts and sit them on top of the rice.

Per serving 591 kcals, **protein** 53.2g, **carbohydrate** 67.4g, **fat** 14.1g, **saturated fat** 3.9g, **fibre** 3.5g, **salt** 1.7g

Lemon and thyme chicken with roast potatoes and olives

30 minutes | serves 2 | easy

3 tbsp olive oil
2 large floury potatoes,
    peeled and cut into
    2cm cubes
14 Kalamata olives, pitted
½ onion, thinly sliced
4 sprigs of thyme, leaves
    stripped from 2 sprigs
2 skinless chicken breasts
1 lemon, quartered
3 tbsp mayonnaise, with a
    squeeze of lemon juice
    or ½ crushed garlic clove
salt and freshly ground
    black pepper

If olives aren't a family favourite, try replacing them with capers. Serve with lots of green veggies.

Preheat the oven to 220°C/Fan 200°C/Gas 7 and put a shallow, non-stick baking tray with 2 tablespoons of the oil in the oven. Bring a pan of water to the boil and cook the potatoes for about 5 minutes, until just tender, then drain thoroughly. Remove the tray from the oven, toss the potatoes in the hot oil, add the olives and the onion to the tray and season. Bake on the top shelf of the oven for 20 minutes, until crisp and golden.

Meanwhile, heat a griddle pan or heavy frying pan. Mix the thyme leaves with the remaining olive oil. Slice the chicken breasts in half horizontally, but not all the way through, and open them out like books. Brush the chicken with the thyme-infused oil and season generously. Put the chicken breasts on the griddle or frying pan, squeeze over the lemon quarters, then leave the lemons, cut-side down, on the griddle. Cook the chicken for 3–4 minutes on each side, until grill-marked (if using the griddle) and cooked through.

Serve the chicken with a squeeze of lemon juice from the lemon grilled with the chicken, the roasties, and a dollop of mayonnaise flavoured with lemon juice or garlic. Garnish with the leftover thyme sprigs.

Per serving 819 kcals, **protein** 44.3g, **carbohydrate** 27.9g, **fat** 58.8g, **saturated fat** 9.1g, **fibre** 2.8g, **salt** 1.6g

Chicken hot wings with blue cheese slaw and skinny fries

1½ hours, plus marinating | serves 2 | easy

400g floury potatoes,
  peeled and cut into
  skinny lengths
500g chicken wings, halved
  at the joint and tips
  removed
50g butter, melted
2–3 tbsp hot pepper sauce
½ tbsp paprika
¼ tsp celery salt
olive oil
salt and freshly ground
  black pepper

For the blue cheese slaw

50g blue cheese (such as
  Dolcelatte), crumbled
100ml half-fat soured
  cream
1 tbsp mayonnaise
1 small white cabbage,
  cored and shredded
½ small red onion, thinly
  sliced

These spicy wings and accompanying blue cheese slaw are an American game-day classic. Adjust the quantity to your party size, and serve with sticks of celery and plenty of napkins!

Put the potatoes into a bowl of cold, salted water and leave for 30 minutes.

Toss the chicken wings with the melted butter, hot pepper sauce, paprika and celery salt, cover and leave to marinate for 30 minutes.

To make the slaw, mash the blue cheese, soured cream and mayonnaise together in a bowl. Toss with the shredded cabbage and red onion, season and leave to sit until you need it. Preheat the oven to 200°C/Fan 180°C/Gas 6.

Drain the potatoes and dry thoroughly on kitchen paper. Toss with a good splash of olive oil and spread on a non-stick baking tray in a single layer. Put the tray on the top half of the oven and cook for 50–55 minutes, giving them a stir occasionally. Season them when cooked.

Put the marinated wings on a separate baking tray, sit them below the fries and cook for 40–45 minutes until crisp and golden.

Toss the slaw again, then serve with the wings and fries.

Per serving 971 kcals, **protein** 48g, **carbohydrate** 49.3g, **fat** 64.7g, **saturated fat** 26g, **fibre** 7.6g, **salt** 2.9g

Chicken braised with cider and bacon

50 minutes | serves 4 | easy

1 tbsp olive oil

4 chicken legs

4 thick-cut smoked back
  bacon rashers, chopped
  into lardons

1 onion, halved and sliced

1 tbsp plain flour

450ml dry cider

1 heaped tsp Dijon
  mustard

1 small Savoy cabbage,
  cored and shredded

25g butter

salt and freshly ground
  black pepper

We at *olive* love this easy chicken recipe with a delicious, cidery sauce. It's also impressive as a dinner party meal.

Preheat the oven to 190°C/Fan 170°C/Gas 5. Heat the oil in a roasting tin or large flameproof casserole over a medium heat. Add the chicken legs and cook for 3–4 minutes on each side, until browned all over. Remove from the tin or casserole.

Add the bacon and onion to the tin or casserole and cook for 3–4 minutes, stirring occasionally, until golden. Stir in the flour and cook for 1 minute, then gradually add the cider. Simmer for 2 minutes, then stir in the mustard.

Sit the chicken legs back in the roasting tin or casserole and cover with foil. Transfer the tin to the oven and bake for 35–40 minutes, or until the chicken is cooked through.

Meanwhile, steam the cabbage until tender. Toss with the butter, season and serve with the chicken.

Per serving 536 kcals, **protein** 38.1g, **carbohydrate** 13.4g, **fat** 35.4g, **saturated fat** 12.1g, **fibre** 5.2g, **salt** 1.96g

Pot pie

1 hour 10 minutes | serves 4 | easy

50g butter

2 small leeks, washed, trimmed and sliced into small chunks

2 tbsp plain flour, plus extra for dusting

300ml milk

1 tsp Dijon mustard

150ml single cream

300g cooked chicken, turkey or ham, torn into chunks (discard any fat or gristle)

small bunch of tarragon, finely chopped

500g block of puff pastry

1 egg, beaten

salt and freshly ground black pepper

Once you've made the creamy leek sauce for the pie, add any cooked meat you fancy – or even add some cooked mushrooms and squash for a veggie version. You can also make two pies and freeze one for an even quicker mid-week meal.

Preheat the oven to 190°C/Fan 170°C/Gas 5. Melt the butter in a shallow, wide pan. Add the leeks and cook for 10 minutes, until really soft. Sprinkle over the flour and cook, stirring, for a few minutes. Gradually add the milk, stirring continuously, until the sauce thickens. Stir in the mustard and cream, then add the meat, seasoning and tarragon. Mix well then tip the pie filling into an ovenproof pie dish.

Roll out the pastry on a lightly floured surface until it is large enough to cover the pie dish, drape it over the top of the filling and crimp the edges. Use the tip of a knife to create a vent in the centre of the pastry (to allow steam to escape), and decorate the top of the pie with pastry trimmings. Glaze with the egg wash and season with a little salt.

Bake for 25–30 minutes until golden. Remove from the oven and serve with peas or other green veg.

Per serving 883 kcals, **protein** 34.4g, **carbohydrate** 47.6g, **fat** 63g, **saturated fat** 31.4g, **fibre** 2.7g, **salt** 1.91g

Crayfish, chicken and rabbit pie

1 hour 30 minutes | serves 2 | a little effort

2 chicken thighs, bone in
and skin removed and
discarded
1 rabbit leg (or 100–150g
diced rabbit meat or
2 more chicken thighs)
3 tbsp plain flour, plus
extra for dusting
2 tbsp sunflower oil
1 small onion, chopped
150ml medium cider
500ml chicken stock
4 tbsp double cream
1 sprig of tarragon, leaves
finely chopped
100–150g crayfish tails,
cooked
200g shortcrust pastry
1 egg, beaten
salt and freshly ground
black pepper

A surf and turf twist on a classic pie that is just as delicious if you leave out the rabbit.

Toss the chicken thighs and rabbit leg with 2 tablespoons of the flour and season. Heat 1 tablespoon of the oil in a flameproof casserole and brown the meat on all sides over a medium heat. Lift out the meat, add the remaining oil and the onion and fry until softened. Add the remaining flour and stir well. Gradually add the cider, stirring continuously and scraping up any sticky bits from the bottom of the pan as it comes to the boil, then add the stock, return the meat to the pan, and bring to a simmer.

Cover and cook for 40–45 minutes until both meats are tender. Lift out the thighs and leg, then remove the meat from the bones in big chunks, meanwhile boil the cooking liquid to reduce it by about a third. Preheat the oven to 200°C/Fan 180°C/Gas 6.

Stir the cream and tarragon into the sauce and taste for seasoning, then stir the meat back in and add the crayfish. Spoon everything into an ovenproof pie dish or baking dish.

Roll out the pastry on a lightly floured surface until it is big enough to cover the pie dish. Stick it on with beaten egg, trim the edges then crimp. Use the tip of a knife to create a vent in the centre of the pastry (to allow steam to escape), and decorate the top of the pie with pastry trimmings. Brush with more egg wash, season with a little salt, and bake for 25 minutes until golden. Remove from the oven and serve with a lightly dressed salad or lots of green veg.

Per serving 1,189 kcals, **protein** 51.1g, **carbohydrate** 73.3g, **fat** 70.5g, **saturated fat** 24.8g, **fibre** 5.6g, **salt** 2.4g

Chicken saltimbocca with green beans and shallots

30 minutes | serves 2 | easy

300g green beans, trimmed
4 small or 2 large chicken thigh fillets
4–8 small sage leaves
4 slices of Parma ham
1 tbsp plain flour, well seasoned
50g butter
2 shallots, finely chopped
100ml white wine
100ml chicken stock
salt and freshly ground black pepper

Saltimbocca means 'jump in the mouth' in Italian. This quick supper of juicy chicken wrapped in Parma ham then pan-fried in butter, shallots and white wine is perfect served on a bed of green beans.

Preheat the oven to 200°C/Fan 180°C/Gas 6. Blanch the green beans in boiling water for 3 minutes then rinse in cold water and drain.

Put the chicken pieces between 2 pieces of cling film and gently bash them out with a meat hammer or rolling pin to thin them a little. Remove the cling film and lay a couple of sage leaves on the smooth side of each thigh, then wrap each thigh in a piece of Parma ham. Dust each piece in seasoned flour. Heat 20g of the butter in a large non-stick frying pan. Cook the chicken for 2–3 minutes on each side, until golden, then transfer the chicken to an ovenproof baking dish and bake in the oven for 10 minutes.

Add a little more butter to the pan and, while the chicken is cooking, fry the shallots for 2 minutes. Add the wine and stock and boil hard until reduced and syrupy. Whisk in the remaining butter, then add the beans and stir to heat through.

Divide the beans between two plates and lay the chicken on top.

Per serving 551 kcals, **protein** 53.2g, **carbohydrate** 11.8g, **fat** 30.8g, **saturated fat** 16.5g, **fibre** 3.6g, **salt** 3.22g

Chicken Kiev

45 minutes, plus chilling | serves 2 | easy

25g butter, softened, plus
  2 tsp for frying
75g dried breadcrumbs
2 large skinless chicken
  breasts
25g soft cream cheese
small handful of wild garlic
  leaves, finely chopped (or
  2 large garlic cloves,
  crushed and mixed with
  1 tbsp finely chopped
  parsley)
2 tbsp plain flour
2 eggs, lightly beaten
salt and freshly ground
  black pepper
salad and shoestring fries,
  to serve

Home-made chicken Kiev is quick and easy to make, and is the best mid-week retro meal. This recipe has a filling of cream cheese, butter and wild garlic. Serve with salad and shoestring fries on the side if you like.

Melt the butter for frying in a frying pan and toast the breadcrumbs until crisp and golden, then transfer them to a wide, shallow bowl and set aside to cool.

Using a small, sharp knife, poke a hole into the side of each chicken breast at the thickest point. Carefully wiggle the knife inside, cutting a large pocket inside the breasts being careful not to widen the hole or poke the knife out at another point.

Beat the softened butter, cream cheese and wild garlic (or garlic and parsley mix) together with some seasoning, then use your fingers to push half the mixture into each breast pocket.

Put the flour and eggs in two separate shallow, wide bowls. Dip each breast in the flour to coat, followed by the egg, then finally into the toasted breadcrumbs to fully coat. Transfer the breasts to a plate, cover, and chill for at least 1 hour (or make the day before and leave in the fridge overnight).

To cook, heat the oven to 200°C/Fan 180°C /Gas 6. Sit the chicken on a non-stick baking tray and cook for 25 minutes, or until cooked through (check by poking a skewer into the centre of the thickest part of the breast – it should feel piping hot and no pinkness remaining). Serve with a salad and shoestring or skinny fries.

Per serving 588 kcals, **protein** 45.7g, **carbohydrate** 43.6g, **fat** 25.9g, **saturated fat** 14.1g, **fibre** 1.2g, **salt** 1.1g

Lemon buttermilk chicken with a piccata sauce

45 minutes, plus marinating | serves 2 | a little effort

2 skinless chicken breasts
1 sprig of rosemary, leaves removed and finely chopped
150ml buttermilk
grated juice and zest of 1 lemon
3 garlic cloves, 2 peeled and bruised and 1 finely chopped
80g panko breadcrumbs
sunflower oil, for frying
1 banana shallot, sliced
200ml chicken stock
small handful of flat-leaf parsley, roughly chopped
1 heaped tbsp capers, rinsed and drained
20g salted butter, chilled and cubed
salt and freshly ground black pepper
baby gem lettuce, mayonnaise and lemon wedges, to serve

Buttermilk chicken may not sound healthy, but the chicken is flattened so the dish goes much further. Serve with baby gem lettuce and lemon for squeezing.

Put the chicken breasts between two sheets of non-stick baking paper and, using a rolling pin or meat hammer, flatten them out to approximately 1cm in thickness. Put the flattened breasts in a ziplock bag and add the rosemary, buttermilk, 2 tablespoons of lemon juice and the bruised garlic cloves. Season well, make sure the chicken is completely coated in the buttermilk mixture, and leave to marinate in the fridge for at least 2 hours, or overnight.

Remove the chicken from the marinade and shake off any excess before coating each piece in the breadcrumbs.

Pour the oil into a frying pan to a depth of about 0.5cm and heat over a medium-high heat and fry the chicken for 6–8 minutes, until golden and cooked through, turning once. Transfer the chicken to a plate lined with kitchen paper, then sprinkle with a little salt and keep warm. Clean out the pan then add another tablespoon of oil.

To make the piccata sauce, add the shallot and chopped garlic to the pan and fry until golden. Add the stock and simmer until reduced by half. Stir through the remaining lemon juice with the zest, parsley and capers.

Finish the sauce by whisking in the butter. Season and serve the chicken with the piccata sauce, gem lettuce leaves, a dollop of mayonnaise and lemon wedges for squeezing over.

Per serving 521 kcals, **protein** 41.6g, **carbohydrate** 34.8g, **fat** 23.5g, **saturated fat** 7.5g, **fibre** 2.7g **salt** 1.9g

Piri-piri chicken with herb coleslaw

45 minutes, plus marinating | serves 4 | easy

8 boneless, skinless
chicken thighs
½ small white cabbage,
shredded
4 carrots, peeled and
grated
1 red onion, thinly sliced
3 tbsp mayonnaise
2 tbsp white wine vinegar
small bunch of coriander,
leaves chopped
salt and freshly ground
black pepper

**For the piri-piri
marinade**
4 red chillies, finely
chopped (deseeded
if you like)
juice of 2 limes
2 garlic cloves, crushed
1 tsp ground coriander
1 tsp ground cinnamon
1 tsp ground ginger

Make your own mid-week takeaway with this fiery piri-piri chicken.

Put the chicken and marinade ingredients in a bowl and toss together. Cover and leave to marinate in the fridge for 2 hours if possible, or at least 15 minutes.

Preheat the oven to 200°C/Fan 180°C/Gas 6. Put the cabbage, carrots and onion in a bowl. Whisk the mayonnaise and vinegar together, then add the mixture to the vegetables, toss and season well.

Remove the chicken from the marinade and place it on a rack over a roasting tin and roast for 30–40 minutes, until golden brown and cooked through. Toss the coriander into the coleslaw and serve with the chicken.

Per serving 580 kcals, **protein** 45.1g, **carbohydrate** 14.3g, **fat** 38.5g, **saturated fat** 11.3g, **fibre** 3.9g, **salt** 1.29g

Chicken and cashew curry with coconut lime noodles

30 minutes | serves 4 | easy

1 tbsp sunflower oil

4 skinless chicken breasts, cut into bite-sized chunks

1 large onion, halved and sliced

6cm piece of fresh root ginger, peeled and finely grated

1 garlic clove, crushed

1 tbsp garam masala

100g cashew nuts, toasted and roughly chopped

400ml can of coconut milk

2 tbsp water

200g rice noodles

1 tbsp fish sauce

1 tbsp palm sugar or golden caster sugar

2 limes, 1 zested and juiced, 1 cut into wedges

salt and freshly ground black pepper

This zesty dish makes a quick mid-week meal. The cashews add a satisfying crunch while the lime gives the dish tanginess. You could serve it with rice, but the coconut lime noodles complement the curry very well.

Heat the oil in a frying pan and cook the chicken until browned (but not cooked through), then remove and set aside. Add the onion, ginger and garlic to the pan and cook until soft, then stir in the garam masala and cashews and cook for a further 2 minutes. Return the chicken to the pan and add half the coconut milk and the water. Season, bring up to a simmer and cook for 10 minutes.

Meanwhile, cook the rice noodles according to the packet instructions, then drain and rinse under cold running water. Place a small pan over a medium heat and add the remaining coconut milk, the fish sauce, sugar, lime zest and juice. Stir until the sugar has melted. Add the drained noodles and heat through.

Serve the chicken and cashew curry with the noodles and wedges of lime to squeeze over the top.

Per serving 721 kcals, **protein** 39.8g, **carbohydrate** 57.4g, **fat** 34.9g, **saturated fat** 18.2g, **fibre** 3.2g, **salt** 1g

Italian chicken and rosemary stew

1½ hours | serves 4 | easy

olive oil, for frying
6 skinless chicken thigh
   fillets (about 500g),
   quartered
2 onions, thinly sliced
2 garlic cloves, crushed
2 sprigs of rosemary, leaves
   stripped and finely
   chopped
1 tbsp balsamic vinegar
2 tbsp pearled spelt
500ml chicken stock
250g waxy potatoes such
   as Charlotte, peeled and
   quartered
salt and freshly ground
   pepper
small bunch of parsley,
   chopped, to serve

Made with easy-to-source ingredients, this warming stew is perfect for winter. Serve with crusty bread if you like.

Preheat the oven to 190°C/Fan 170°C/Gas 5. Heat a little olive oil in a frying pan, add the chicken thighs and cook until browned.

Remove the chicken and set aside, then add the onions to the pan and cook until softened. Add the garlic and rosemary and cook for a minute, add the balsamic vinegar and cook for a further minute, then add the spelt, stock, potatoes and the chicken. Season, bring to a simmer then transfer to an ovenproof dish, cover and put it in the oven for 1 hour. Scatter over the parsley to serve.

Per serving 257 kcals, **protein** 29.4g, **carbohydrate** 21.4g, **fat** 6.6g, **saturated fat** 1.7g, **fibre** 2.3g, **salt** 1.26g

Roasted tarragon chicken with carrots, leeks and new potatoes

1 hour 30 minutes | serves 4 | easy

50g butter, softened
1 garlic clove, crushed
1 tbsp chopped tarragon
1 tbsp chopped parsley
grated zest of 1 lemon
1 medium chicken (about
  1.5kg)
1kg new potatoes,
  scrubbed
500g young carrots
500g small leeks, washed,
  trimmed and halved
  lengthways
salt and freshly ground
  black pepper

This one-pot chicken recipe makes an easy-to-prepare mid-week roast. It is delicious with any herbs you have to hand, so if you can't get hold of tarragon, replace it with rosemary, thyme, sage, or even a mixture of herbs.

Preheat the oven to 200°C/Fan 180°C/Gas 6. Beat the butter, garlic, herbs and lemon zest together in a small bowl, and season well.

Using your hands, carefully loosen the skin over the chicken breast, starting from the neck end. Spread two-thirds of the herb butter between the breast and the skin, then smooth the skin back down. Place the chicken in a roasting tin, season and roast for 1 hour 15 minutes, or until the juices run clear when the thigh is tested with a skewer.

Meanwhile, boil the potatoes and carrots in salted water for 5 minutes. Drain well and tip them into another roasting tin, add the remaining herby butter and roast above the chicken for 30 minutes, or until tender.

Cook the leeks for 2 minutes in boiling, salted water, drain well and add them to the other veggies. Return the tin to the oven for another 15 minutes. Serve the chicken carved into thick slices, with the roasted veggies, and the pan juices poured over the top.

Per serving 739 kcals, **protein** 64.9g, **carbohydrate** 15.9g, **fat** 43.2g, **saturated fat** 21.3g, **fibre** 1.9g, **salt** 1.86g

Soft chicken tacos with black bean salsa

45 minutes | serves 2 | easy

4 skinless chicken thigh
  fillets
1 tsp mild chilli powder
2 tsp ground cumin, plus
  an extra pinch
1 tbsp olive oil
juice of 2 limes
1 small ripe avocado,
  peeled, stoned and diced
400g can of black beans,
  drained and rinsed
10 cherry tomatoes,
  quartered
½ small red onion, finely
  chopped
1 chilli, finely chopped
4–6 flour tortillas, warmed,
  to serve
small bunch of coriander,
  leaves chopped, to serve

The chicken is marinated in lime for these fresh tacos. For a healthier option, try making your taco with lettuce wraps instead of the flour tortilla.

Toss the chicken with the spices, olive oil and half the lime juice, and season generously. Cover and set aside for 15 minutes to marinate.

Meanwhile, make the salsa – mix the avocado, black beans, tomatoes, onion and chilli in a bowl with the remaining lime juice and a pinch of ground cumin.

Heat the grill and cook the chicken under the grill for 10–12 minutes, turning it once or twice until the thighs are browned and cooked through. Remove and set aside to rest for a couple of minutes, then slice and serve with the black bean salsa and warmed tortillas, sprinkled with the coriander.

Per serving 508 kcals, **protein** 51.1g, **carbohydrate** 27.1g, **fat** 22.3g, **saturated fat** 4.1g, **fibre** 8.4g, **salt** 0.57g

Chicken chilli bowl

45 minutes | serves 2 | easy

1 tbsp groundnut oil
4 skinless chicken thigh
   fillets, quartered
1 onion, chopped
1 green pepper, deseeded
   and finely chopped
1 tsp smoked paprika
½ tsp hot chilli powder
1 tsp cumin seeds, toasted
400g can of chopped
   tomatoes
400g can of pinto beans,
   rinsed and drained
200ml chicken stock
100g green beans,
   trimmed and cut
   into pieces
salt and freshly ground
   black pepper
natural yoghurt, to serve
plain tortilla chips, to serve

This chilli is packed with beans and veg so you don't need rice, just a few tortilla chips.

Heat the oil in a saucepan and brown the chicken all over. Remove the chicken from the pan and set to one side, then cook the onion in the same pan for 5–7 minutes, until golden and softened. Add the pepper and cook for a few minutes, until softened, then return the chicken to the pan.

Stir in all the spices and cook for 1 minute, then tip in the tomatoes, pinto beans and chicken stock. Simmer for 15 minutes, season, then add the green beans and simmer for another 10 minutes. Divide the chilli between two bowls and serve with a spoonful of yoghurt and a handful of tortilla chips.

Per serving 435 kcals, **protein** 49.3g, **carbohydrate** 27.4g, **fat** 12.7g, **saturated fat** 2.9g, **fibre** 9.1g, **salt** 1.8g

Chicken enchiladas

55 minutes | serves 3 | easy

1 tbsp olive oil
1 red onion, finely
　chopped
1 garlic clove, chopped
6 jalapeños from a jar,
　finely chopped (or more
　to suit your taste)
400g can of chopped
　tomatoes
6 corn tortillas
200g Cheddar cheese,
　grated
2 large cooked chicken
　breasts, or the equivalent
　of leftover roast chicken,
　shredded
small bunch of coriander,
　chopped
215g can of refried beans
salt and freshly ground
　black pepper
200ml soured cream,
　to serve

This Tex-Mex favourite is a comforting dish that's guaranteed to pep-up your evening because not only does it taste so good, the chilli prompts an endorphin rush too.

Heat the olive oil in a saucepan. Add the onion and fry gently for 3–5 minutes. As it begins to soften, add the garlic and about a third of the jalapeños. Continue to cook, stirring occasionally, until the onion and garlic are soft and translucent. Add the tomatoes, half-fill the tomato can with water, swish it around, then tip it into the pan. Season. Simmer for about 15 minutes, until the sauce is thick and glossy. Preheat the oven to 200°C/Fan 180°C/Gas 6.

While the sauce is cooking, wrap the tortillas in foil and warm them in the oven for 10 minutes.

Now assemble the enchiladas. Set a good third of the grated cheese aside. Spread 1 teaspoon of the tomato sauce all over one side of each warm tortilla. Divide the shredded chicken and remaining grated cheese into 6 portions and add a portion of chicken in a thick line down the middle of each tortilla. Top each one with a portion of cheese and a sprinkling of jalapeños and coriander (keeping some coriander aside to serve). Then add 1 rounded teaspoon of refried beans to each. (Don't overdo the beans – you can serve what's left as a side.) Roll the edges over to make 6 long tubes. Reduce the oven temperature to 190°C/Fan 170°C/Gas 5.

Put the enchiladas, seam-side down, in a ceramic baking dish. Pour the remaining tomato mix over the top, sprinkle with the reserved cheese, and cook for 20–25 minutes until the cheese has melted and the enchiladas are piping hot. Serve sprinkled with chopped coriander and dollops of soured cream.

Per serving 683 kcals, **protein** 49.9g, **carbohydrate** 30.4g **fat** 38.7g, **saturated fat** 17g, **fibre** 6.6g, **salt** 2.4g

Budin Azteca

50 minutes | serves 2 | easy

4 corn tortillas

2 tsp olive oil

1 onion, chopped

2 garlic cloves, chopped

1 red pepper, deseeded
   and chopped

1 green pepper, deseeded
   and chopped

400g can of chopped
   tomatoes

2 tsp chipotle paste, or
   a good shake of chipotle
   Tabasco

200g cooked chicken, cut
   into bite-sized chunks

75ml soured cream

100g Cheddar cheese,
   grated

4 jalapeños from a jar,
   chopped

salt and freshly ground
   black pepper

Budin Azteca, or tortilla lasagne, is a spicy, Mexican twist on your classic lasagne. Serve with a side of rice and a dollop of soured cream.

Preheat the oven to 190°C/Fan 170°C/Gas 5. Brush the tortillas on both sides lightly with 1 teaspoon of the olive oil, then toast in a large dry frying pan over a medium heat until both sides are crisp and browned.

Fry the onion and garlic in the remaining olive oil until softened, then add the peppers and cook until they soften a little. Add the tomatoes and chipotle paste or Tabasco and simmer for 20 minutes until thickened. Season.

Put a tortilla in the bottom of an ovenproof baking dish or small ovenproof frying pan. Spread over a third of the sauce, a third of the chicken, 1 tablespoon of the soured cream and a quarter of the cheese. Repeat twice, with two more tortillas, sprinkling with jalapeños as you go, then add the last tortilla and top it with soured cream and cheese only. Use a bit more cheese if you need to, to get a generous top layer. Bake for 20–30 minutes, until it is bubbling and golden on top.

Per serving 675 kcals, **protein** 47.9g, **carbohydrate** 34.9g, **fat** 37.4g, **saturated fat** 18.4g, **fibre** 6.8g, **salt** 1.6g

Entertaining

Chicken filo parcels with carrot and watercress salad

30 minutes | serves 4 | easy

3 cooked skinless chicken
  breasts, roughly chopped
½ tbsp Baharat spice blend
  (or use a mix of paprika,
  ground coriander and
  ground black pepper)
1 tbsp peeled and grated
  fresh root ginger
6 spring onions, finely
  chopped
15g coriander, leaves
  chopped
1 lemon
2 large sheets filo pastry
olive oil, for brushing
2 tsp sesame seeds
2 carrots, cut into
  matchsticks
2 large handfuls of
  watercress, roughly torn
salt and freshly ground
  black pepper
150g natural yoghurt,
  to serve

This is a great way to control portions, and you get a satisfying crunch from the filo pastry. These party-sized parcels also make handy starters.

Preheat the oven to 200°C/Fan 180°C/Gas 6. Mix the chicken with the spice blend, ginger, spring onions and coriander in a bowl. Add a squeeze of lemon juice and some seasoning and mix.

Brush the pastry sheets with 2 tablespoons of olive oil and cut them in half lengthways. Divide the chicken mix between the four pieces, putting the mixture at the bottom of each and folding the bottom edge up to meet one side to start the shape of the triangle. Keep folding upwards from one side to the other until you reach the top. Brush with a little more oil and sprinkle over 1 teaspoon of the sesame seeds. Bake for 15 minutes, until brown and crisp.

Mix the carrots with the watercress, remaining juice from the lemon, the remaining sesame seeds and a little olive oil and seasoning. Serve the filo parcels with yoghurt and the carrot and watercress salad.

Per serving 287 kcals, **protein** 31.9g, **carbohydrate** 15g, **fat** 11.5g, **saturated fat** 2.3g, **fibre** 2.3g, **salt** 0.35g

Chicken and pistachio pilaf

30 minutes | serves 4 | easy

1 tbsp olive oil

2 large onions, halved and thinly sliced

400g skinless chicken thigh fillets, cut into 3cm pieces

2 tbsp dried cherries, chopped

¼ tsp ground allspice

1 cinnamon stick

250g basmati rice, rinsed

400ml chicken stock

3 tbsp pistachio nuts, chopped

salt and freshly ground black pepper

natural yoghurt, to serve (optional)

With cinnamon, allspice, cherries and pistachios, this pilaf has plenty of flavour. Serve as a main with a big salad, or make it without the chicken and serve it to your guests as a side dish.

Heat the olive oil in a large, heavy saucepan. Add the onion and season. Cook for 12–15 minutes, until very golden and crisp at the edges. Remove half the onion, drain on kitchen paper and set aside.

Add the chicken, cherries, allspice and cinnamon to the pan and cook for 5 minutes. Add the rice along with the stock, bring to a boil, then reduce the heat and simmer, covered, for 12 minutes, until the liquid is all absorbed. Stir the nuts through the rice and scatter over the crispy onions. Serve with a dollop of natural yoghurt, if you like.

Per serving 429 kcals, **protein** 28.5g, **carbohydrate** 65g, **fat** 8g, **saturated fat** 1.7g, **fibre** 2.5g, **salt** 1g

Prosciutto-wrapped chicken with garlic mash

50 minutes | serves 6 | easy

12 chicken thighs, bone-in
and skin removed and
discarded
24 slices of prosciutto
24 sage leaves
olive oil, for drizzling
1.5kg floury potatoes,
peeled and cut into
3cm chunks
75g butter
2 garlic cloves, crushed
splash of milk, for mashing
salt and freshly ground
black pepper
450g green beans, cooked,
to serve

Stuffed chicken breast is a classic dinner party pleaser. Wrapping the chicken in prosciutto helps lock in the juicy chicken flavour and cooking chicken on the bone gives it a nice shape.

Preheat the oven to 200°C/Fan 180°C/Gas 6. Wrap each chicken thigh in 2 slices of prosciutto, tucking in some sage leaves as you go. Season and drizzle with a little olive oil, then put them on a baking tray and cook for 40 minutes, until crisp and cooked through.

While the chicken is cooking, boil the potatoes in salted water until tender. Melt the butter in a frying pan and cook the garlic gently for 3 minutes. Drain the potatoes, return them to the pan and mash with the garlic butter and a splash of milk. Serve the chicken with the garlic mash and some green beans.

Per serving 496 kcals, **protein** 37g, **carbohydrate** 41.1g, **fat** 19.6g, **saturated fat** 9.3g, **fibre** 3.3g, **salt** 2.2g

Fideua with king prawns, chicken and mussels

1 hour | serves 4 | tricky but worth it

olive oil, for frying

350g fideua pasta

2 skinless chicken breasts,
   cut into bite-sized pieces

2 garlic cloves, finely sliced

1 tsp smoked paprika

a good pinch of saffron

1 small tomato, chopped

500g mussels, cleaned

150g peas, blanched

150g broad beans, podded
   and blanched

10 basil leaves, torn

For the aioli

5 garlic cloves, peeled

1 tsp salt

4 egg yolks

180ml light olive oil

1 tsp smoked paprika

For the stock

12 raw, shell-on king prawns

olive oil, for frying

½ small onion, roughly
   chopped

1 tomato, roughly chopped

3 garlic cloves, roughly
   chopped

1.5 litres water

1 chicken stock cube

1 star anise

Fideua is a Spanish dish similar to paella, but it uses short strands of pasta instead of rice (you can find it in Spanish delis or online). You can use paella rice instead, but the cooking time will need to be increased. Let people help themselves and serve it straight from the pan with lots of crusty bread and the punchy aioli. The stock is simple to make and is an important part of the dish so try not to skip this step.

To make the aioli, crush the garlic with the salt in a pestle and mortar then transfer them to a bowl. Whisk in the egg yolks then gradually whisk in the olive oil until the mixture has thickened. Finally, whisk in the smoked paprika. Cover and chill until needed.

To make the stock, pull the heads off the prawns and peel off the shells, then put the peeled prawns back in the fridge. Place a pan over a medium heat and add 1 tablespoon of olive oil. Add the onion, tomato, garlic, and prawn shells and heads. Sizzle everything for 3–4 minutes, then pour in the water, crumble in the stock cube and add the star anise. Simmer for 30 minutes then fish out the star anise and pulse everything in a food processor or blender. Strain the stock through a fine sieve and measure out 1.2 litres.

Heat 3 tablespoons of olive oil in a large, shallow pan then tip in the fideua pasta and stir, letting it turn gently golden in the heat of the oil. Add the chicken, garlic, smoked paprika and saffron and let them sizzle in the oil for 30 seconds, then add the tomato and three-quarters of the stock and bring to a simmer. Cook for 10 minutes, stirring occasionally. Add the peeled prawns, mussels and the remaining stock and continue to simmer for another 5 minutes. Taste and stir as you go: the pasta should be cooked but not mushy and the stock should be almost totally absorbed. Season. Once the mussels are open and the prawns are pink, add the peas and broad beans to heat through. Stir in the basil and serve with the aioli and lots of crusty bread.

Per serving 518 kcals, **protein** 37.6g, **carbohydrate** 53.6g, **fat** 16.2g, **saturated fat** 2.1g, **fibre** 6g, **salt** 2.9g

Baked Spanish rice with chicken and chorizo

1 hour | serves 4–6 | easy

4 tbsp olive oil

12 whole chicken thighs
 and drumsticks

2 red peppers, deseeded
 and sliced

200g cooking chorizo,
 cut into small chunks

1 large onion, roughly
 chopped

4 garlic cloves, crushed

2 tbsp hot smoked paprika

1 tsp chilli flakes

1.3 litres chicken stock

375g paella rice

salt and freshly ground
 black pepper

2 tbsp chopped flat-leaf
 parsley, to garnish

1 lemon, halved

A spicy Spanish one pot. Made with chicken and chorizo and plenty of hot smoked paprika, this is a gutsy rice dish that is similar to paella but easier to cook.

Preheat the oven to 180°C/Fan 160°C/Gas 4. Heat the oil in a very large, wide, shallow ovenproof pan, season the chicken and brown it all over in batches. Remove the chicken and set aside, then add the peppers and chorizo to the same pan and cook over a medium heat until the peppers begin to soften.

Add the onion and garlic and cook gently until the onion is soft. Stir in the paprika and chilli flakes and cook for 1 minute, stirring, then add the chicken stock. Put the chicken pieces back in the pan, bring the stock to a simmer and cook, covered, over a gentle heat for 15 minutes.

Pour the rice all around the chicken and season – if you don't have a big enough pan, you can transfer everything to a roasting tin.

Transfer the pan to the oven and cook for 20–25 minutes, or until the stock has been absorbed and the top is golden. Cover the dish with foil and leave to sit for 5 minutes, then scatter with the parsley and squeeze lemon juice over the top before serving.

Per serving 717 kcals, protein 45.3g, carbohydrate 55.6g, fat 34.8g, saturated fat 9.9g, fibre 5g, salt 1.3g

Chicken cacciatore

1 hour 10 minutes | serves 4 | easy

1 large chicken, jointed
  into 8 pieces
2 tbsp olive oil
1 onion, finely chopped
2 garlic cloves, sliced
70g diced pancetta
1 glass of red wine (about
  175ml)
2 x 400g cans cherry
  tomatoes or chopped
  tomatoes
2 tbsp small capers, rinsed
  and drained
10 black olives, pitted and
  halved
handful of basil leaves
salt and freshly ground
  black pepper

This has been one of *olive*'s most popular recipes for years. We think it might just be the best chicken recipe *ever*. Serve with a short pasta such as fusilli, or a big bowl of potatoes roasted with olive oil and rosemary.

Season the chicken all over. Heat the olive oil in a large non-stick frying pan and fry the chicken until golden. Take the chicken out of the pan and set aside, then add the onion and garlic to the pan. Cook gently until the onion is soft. Add the pancetta and cook for 3 minutes, then add the red wine and simmer until it has almost disappeared. Preheat the oven to 190°C/Fan 170°C/Gas 5. Add the tomatoes and season well. Simmer the sauce for 15 minutes until it thickens. Stir in the capers and olives.

Tip the sauce into the bottom of an ovenproof dish and sit the chicken in the sauce. Transfer the dish to the oven and cook for 30–40 minutes, until the chicken is cooked through. Stir in the basil and serve with pasta or roast potatoes.

Per serving 774 kcals, **protein** 61.5g, **carbohydrate** 8.6g, **fat** 52.3g, **saturated fat** 14.2g, **fibre** 2.3g, **salt** 1.9g

Baked chicken with mascarpone and tarragon

45 minutes | serves 8 | easy

300g cherry tomatoes, halved

1 tbsp olive oil, plus extra for drizzling

8 bone-in, skin-on chicken breasts (without wings), trimmed of excess fat

150g mascarpone

2 tsp Dijon mustard

2 tbsp grated Parmesan cheese

small bunch of tarragon, leaves finely chopped

4 tbsp small capers, rinsed and squeezed dry

salt and freshly ground black pepper

You can prepare the chicken for this dish ahead, to be cooked at the last minute, and also cook the tomatoes ahead if you like – just remember to save the juices. Serve with roast baby potatoes and salad.

Heat the oven to 220°C/Fan 200°C/Gas 7. Tip the cherry tomatoes into a baking dish, add the olive oil and season well. Roast for 20 minutes.

Loosen the skin on each chicken breast. Mix 6 tablespoons of the mascarpone with the mustard, Parmesan and half the tarragon and season well. Spread the mixture between the skin and chicken on each breast and smooth the skin back on. Lay the chicken in a single layer in a large baking dish or roasting tin, drizzle a little olive oil over the skin and roast for 20–30 minutes or until the chicken is cooked through and the skin is crisp.

Scoop the tomatoes out of their dish, shaking off the juices and keep them warm. Lift the chicken breasts out of the dish, leaving behind the juices. Add the tomato juices to the chicken juices, along with the remaining mascarpone and tarragon, whisk them together and season again (re-warm if necessary). Heat a little oil and fry the capers until they sizzle. Serve the chicken with the tomatoes, sauce and a sprinkling of capers.

Per serving 437 kcals, **protein** 48.4g, **carbohydrate** 2.2g, **fat** 26.1g, **saturated fat** 10.5g, **fibre** 0.6g, **salt** 0.8g

Chicken with morels, mascarpone and peas

2 hours | serves 4 | easy

1 whole, large chicken
  (about 2.5kg)
3 tbsp butter, plus extra
  for frying
12 small shallots, peeled
180g fresh morels (or 20g
  dried and rehydrated
  morels)
75ml white wine
100g peas
180g mascarpone
salt and freshly ground
  black pepper

Fresh morels, when in season, add a wonderful flavour to this elegant dish. You can also make it year round using dried morels or button mushrooms too.

Heat the oven to 180°C/Fan 160°C/Gas 4. Rub the chicken all over with 2 tablespoons of butter and season it well. Put it in a shallow baking dish that has a little room around the edges and roast for 40 minutes. Remove the dish from the oven, add the shallots to the dish along with the remaining butter and return it to the oven for a further 50 minutes, or until the chicken juices run clear.

Meanwhile, melt a little butter in a frying pan and fry the morels briefly, moving them carefully around the pan so they don't break up. Add the white wine and simmer until it reduces by half, then stir in the peas and take the pan off the heat.

Lift the chicken out of the dish, pouring any juices back into the dish, and transfer the chicken to a serving dish and leave to rest, covered loosely in foil, for 20 minutes. Discard the fat settled on top of the chicken dish, and add the juices and shallots to the morel mixture. When the chicken is rested, reheat the mixture gently, then stir in the mascarpone. Carve the chicken and serve it with the morel sauce.

Per serving 933 kcals, **protein** 81.9g, **carbohydrate** 6.9g, **fat** 62.1g, **saturated fat** 27.8g, **fibre** 3.5g, **salt** 0.8g

Chicken and purple sprouting broccoli pie

1 hour | serves 6 | easy

750ml chicken stock

2 tbsp chopped tarragon leaves

6 skinless, boneless chicken thighs, cut into large pieces

85g butter

85g plain flour

2 tbsp crème fraîche

½ tbsp Dijon mustard

300g purple sprouting broccoli, chopped into bite-sized lengths

salt and freshly ground black pepper

For the topping

6–8 large floury potatoes, peeled and chopped

2–3 tbsp whole milk

large knob of butter

salt and freshly ground black pepper

Topped with mashed potato and in a creamy sauce, this is surely the best way to eat purple sprouting broccoli. Serve with a side of carrots and a leafy salad or all on its own.

Put the chicken stock in a saucepan with half the tarragon and bring it to a simmer, then add the chicken and cook for 4 minutes, or until just cooked through. Lift the chicken out with a slotted spoon and set aside. Strain the stock into a jug. Melt the butter in a pan and add the flour, stir to form a roux and cook for a minute until it bubbles. Take the pan off the heat, whisk in a little of the stock to make a smooth paste, then gradually add the remaining stock. Put the pan back over the heat and simmer until you have a thick, glossy sauce. Stir in the crème fraîche and mustard, then season.

Meanwhile, cook the broccoli in simmering water or in a steamer for 5 minutes or until it is tender. Drain well. Stir the chicken and broccoli into the sauce and transfer the mixture to an ovenproof dish. Preheat the oven to 220°C/Fan 200°C/Gas 7.

Cook the potatoes in simmering salted water until tender. Drain, put them back in the pan with a splash of milk, the butter and plenty of seasoning. Mash well then spoon over the chicken and fluff up the surface of the potato with a fork. Bake for 15 minutes to crisp the top.

Per serving 503 kcals, **protein** 30.8g, **carbohydrate** 52g, **fat** 19g, **saturated fat** 10.6g, **fibre** 7.3g, **salt** 0.9g

Spicy chicken drumsticks

1 hour, plus marinating | makes 8 | easy

4 tbsp tomato ketchup
2 tbsp runny honey
2 tbsp Worcestershire
    sauce
2 garlic cloves, crushed
8 chicken drumsticks
    (about 800g)
salt and freshly ground
    black pepper

This is a sure-fire crowd pleaser. Serve with corn on the cob and coleslaw for a Southern American dish, or as finger food if you're entertaining.

Mix everything together except the chicken in a large bowl. Pull the skin off the drumsticks starting from the widest part, then slash them 2–3 times through the thickest parts with a knife. Toss the drumsticks with the sauce in the bowl and season. Marinate in the fridge for an hour.

Preheat the oven to 200°C/Fan 180°C/Gas 6 and line a roasting tin with foil. Arrange the marinated chicken in a single layer in the prepared tin and brush with half the marinade. Bake for 15 minutes then brush with a little more marinade. Cook for another 30 minutes, brushing with the remaining marinade after 15 minutes. Serve warm or cold with plenty of napkins.

Per serving 101 kcals, **protein** 15.5g, **carbohydrate** 55.4g, **fat** 2.1g, **saturated fat** 0.8g, **fibre** 0.1g, **salt** 0.45g

Tex-Mex chicken with guacamole

30 minutes | serves 4 | easy

4 skinless chicken breasts
juice of 1 lime
olive oil
1 ripe avocado, peeled,
   stoned and chopped
1 red chilli, finely chopped
   (deseeded if you like)
handful of coriander,
   leaves chopped
½ garlic clove, crushed
4 ciabatta buns, split and
   toasted
salt and freshly ground
   black pepper
soft lettuce leaves, to serve
soured cream, to serve
sliced jalapeños from a jar,
   to serve
Tabasco, to serve

These chicken burgers are easy to make, and the guacamole makes a refreshing change to your usual barbecue salad topping. Serve to your guests with grilled corn on the cob and a tomato, onion and lime salad.

Light the barbecue or heat up a griddle pan. Butterfly the chicken breasts (cut them in half horizontally and open them up like a book). Put the butterflied breasts in a dish, season well and drizzle over 1 tablespoon of lime juice, a little olive oil and toss. Leave for 10 minutes.

To make the guacamole, put the avocado, chilli, coriander, garlic and the rest of the lime juice in a bowl, roughly mash together and season.

Grill the chicken on the barbecue or griddle for 2–3 minutes on each side, until cooked. Remove and leave to rest, covered with foil, for 3 minutes. Put some lettuce on the bottom of each bun. Top with the grilled chicken, a dollop of the guacamole, some soured cream and jalapeños. Serve Tabasco on the side for those who want extra heat.

Per serving 478 kcals, **protein** 43.9g, **carbohydrate** 46.2g, **fat** 14.4g, **saturated fat** 2.4g, **fibre** 3.4g, **salt** 1.75g

Buttermilk fried chicken

1 hour, plus marinating | serves 4 | easy

1.5kg chicken thighs and
   drumsticks, skin on, bone
   in, excess skin trimmed
2 x 284ml cartons
   buttermilk
1 onion, sliced
200g plain flour
groundnut oil, for frying
flaked sea salt and freshly
   ground black pepper

For the spice mix
3 tsp paprika
1 tsp garlic salt
1 tsp celery salt
½ tsp cayenne pepper
1 tsp dried thyme
flaked sea salt and freshly
   ground black peper

Soaking the chicken in buttermilk tenderises the meat and helps the crispy coating stick to the chicken. Serve hot to your guests with corn on the cob and mashed potatoes or cold with a salad the following day.

Toss the chicken pieces in a bowl with the buttermilk, onion and some seasoning. Cover and leave to chill for 3–4 hours.

Preheat the oven to 200°C/Fan 180°C/Gas 6. Put a large wire rack in a roasting tin. Combine the ingredients for the spice mix and add them to the flour on a large flat plate. Add a generous amount of seasoning and toss together. Take each piece of marinated chicken and shake, leaving the excess marinade and the onion behind. Toss in the spiced flour to coat.

Heat the groundnut oil to a depth of 2cm, in a large, deep non-stick frying pan until a cube of bread browns in 30 seconds. Carefully add the chicken in batches of 3 or 4 pieces at a time and fry for a few minutes on all sides until lightly golden (don't let them get too dark as they are going to continue to cook in the oven). Carefully transfer each piece of fried chicken to the rack in the roasting tin. When all the pieces have been fried, put them on a low shelf in the oven for 30–35 minutes until cooked through. Serve hot, sprinkled with flaked sea salt and black pepper.

Per serving 509 kcals, **protein** 58g, **carbohydrate** 40g, **fat** 13g, **saturated fat** 3.2g, **fibre** 1.7g, **salt** 3.6g

Sweet chilli chicken and lime skewers

20 minutes | serves 6 | easy

4 large skinless chicken
  breasts, cut into cubes
4 tbsp sweet chilli sauce
1 garlic clove, crushed
juice of 1 lime, plus
  3 limes, halved, to serve
300g cherry tomatoes,
  halved
small bunch of coriander,
  leaves picked
½ small red onion, finely
  sliced
olive oil, for drizzling

These skewers are sweet and tangy, with a bit of a kick too: a sure-fire crowd pleaser at any barbecue.

Light the barbecue, if using. Put the chicken breast cubes, sweet chilli sauce, garlic and lime juice in a bowl, toss and leave to marinate for 10 minutes.

Thread the chicken onto metal or wooden skewers (remember to soak in water first if you use wooden) and barbecue on indirect heat (or chargrill on a griddle pan) for 6–8 minutes, turning until cooked through but not blackened.

Toss the tomatoes, coriander and onion in a bowl with a little olive oil. Griddle or barbecue the lime halves, cut-side down, until caramelised. Serve the skewers with a little tomato salad and a caramelised lime half for squeezing over the top.

Per serving 161 kcals, **protein** 24.6g, **carbohydrate** 4.8g, **fat** 5g, **saturated fat** 0.9g, **fibre** 0.7g, **salt** 0.39g

Roast chicken with peverada sauce

1 hour 50 minutes | serves 4 | easy

1 chicken, jointed into
  8 pieces
olive oil
1 onion, finely chopped
1 garlic clove, unpeeled
1 rosemary sprig, leaves
  finely chopped
4 sage leaves, finely
  chopped
100g chicken livers,
  cleaned and roughly
  chopped
1 Italian sausage, skinned
  and chopped, or 2 slices
  soft salami, chopped
2 anchovies in oil, finely
  chopped
1 tsp golden caster sugar
1 lemon, halved
3 tbsp red wine vinegar
2 handfuls of flat-leaf
  parsley, chopped
salt and freshly ground
  black pepper
radicchio, treviso or red
  endive, dressed, to serve

Peverada sauce is based on a Venetian dish with chicken liver, sausage and anchovies. Serve with a side of pasta and radicchio.

Preheat the oven to 180°C/Fan 160°C/Gas 4. Rub the chicken pieces with a little olive oil and season well. Pour 2 tablespoons of olive oil into a roasting tin that fits the chicken quite snugly in a single layer, add the onion, garlic, rosemary and sage, and put the chicken pieces on top. Roast for 45 minutes, or until golden and cooked through. Lift out the chicken and set it aside to rest, covered, for 10 minutes.

While the chicken is resting, sieve the roasting juices, keeping the onion and herbs. Strain the fat from the juices and pour the juices into a jug.

Heat a frying pan and add the reserved onion and herbs. Add the chicken livers, sausage and anchovies and cook gently until the meat is cooked through. Season, add the sugar, squeeze in the juice from half the lemon and stir in the vinegar and roasting juices. Taste and add more vinegar if the sauce needs it – it should be slightly sweet and sharp. Stir in the parsley. Serve with the chicken and a raddichio salad.

Per serving 623 kcals, **protein** 53.4g, **carbohydrate** 4.3g, **fat** 43.3g, **saturated fat** 11.3g, **fibre** 0.8g, **salt** 0.9g

Pot-roast chicken with leeks

1 hour 45 minutes | serves 4 | easy

2 tbsp olive oil

100g smoked streaky
   bacon, chopped

1 whole chicken (about
   1.6kg)

3 sprigs of thyme

2 large leeks, trimmed and
   thickly sliced

2 celery sticks, trimmed
   and thickly sliced

200ml white wine

200ml chicken stock

salt and freshly ground
   black pepper

For the salsa verde

3 anchovy fillets in oil,
   drained

1 garlic clove, peeled and
   roughly chopped

handful of celery leaves

large handful of flat-leaf
   parsley, leaves chopped

2½ tbsp red wine vinegar

2 tsp finely chopped
   rosemary leaves

2 tsp finely chopped sage
   leaves

120ml extra-virgin olive oil

**Adding salsa verde to your standard roast chicken gives it a lovely
punchy, herby kick. If you don't like anchovies, simply leave them out.**

Preheat the oven to 200°C/Fan 180°C/Gas 6. Heat the oil in a lidded
casserole large enough to hold the chicken. Add the bacon and cook,
stirring, until it begins to brown. Push the bacon to the edges of the pan
and add the chicken, breast-side down. Cook for about 3 minutes on each
side, until golden brown all over, then turn it breast side up to finish.

Add the thyme sprigs, leeks and celery to the pan with the wine and
chicken stock. Season then put the lid on and roast in the oven for
1 hour 30 minutes.

Meanwhile, make the salsa verde by blitzing all the ingredients together in
a food processor to make a textured sauce. Taste and add a little more red
wine vinegar or oil if needed. Serve the chicken, vegetables and roasting
juices with spoonfuls of the salsa verde.

Per serving 771 kcals, **protein** 52.1g, **carbohydrate** 4.2g, **fat** 56.8g, **saturated fat** 14.1g, **fibre** 3.0g, **salt** 1.4 g

Herb-roast chicken

1 hour 45 minutes, plus overnight sitting | serves 4 | easy

1 whole chicken
(about 2kg)
olive oil
2 lemons, cut into quarters
a handful of thyme,
rosemary or tarragon,
depending on preference
1 large onion, cut into fat
discs

Leaving the chicken out overnight really makes a world of difference as it is able to sit in its own juices and becomes extra succulent. This recipe requires few ingredients so makes your weekend roast extra-easy.

The day before you want to cook the chicken, take it out of any wrapping and remove the giblets, sit it in a large ceramic dish (to catch any juices that drip out) and leave it uncovered in the fridge on the lowest shelf.

The next day, take the chicken out of the fridge and let it sit at room temperature for 50 minutes before you start cooking. Heat the oven to 220°C/Fan 200°C/Gas 7.

Brush the chicken with olive oil, season it with salt and pepper inside and out, then put the lemon quarters and a few sprigs of herbs in the cavity.

Put the chicken in a shallow roasting tin on top of the onion discs, add a splash of water to the tin and roast for 20 minutes. Turn the oven down to 180°C/Fan 160°C/Gas 4 and cook for another hour.

Check to see if the chicken is cooked by pushing a skewer into the thigh and checking that the juices run out clear, not pink. Cook for a little longer if you need to, then remove the bird from the oven and leave it to rest for 15 minutes before carving. This lets the juices re-absorb, giving juicy, succulent meat that's easier to carve.

Per serving 553 kcals, **protein** 62.6g, **carbohydrate** 32.5g, **fat** 16.8g, **saturated fat** 4.2g, **fibre** 0.6g, **salt** 0.3g

Flat-grilled chicken with Texas cornbread

2 hours, plus marinating time | serves 4 | a little effort

1 whole chicken (about 1.5kg)
1 tsp smoked paprika
½ tsp chilli powder
1 tsp ground cumin
2 tbsp tomato ketchup
1 tbsp brown sugar
2 tbsp cider vinegar
olive oil
salt and freshly ground black pepper

For the cornbread
75g butter, plus extra for greasing
250ml buttermilk
150ml whole milk
2 eggs
300g polenta
100g self-raising flour
2 tbsp golden caster sugar
1 tsp baking powder

A spicy roast chicken with moist cornbread. Flatten, or spatchcock, this chicken ahead of time and leave it to marinate until you're ready to cook for maximum flavour.

Preheat the oven to 180°C/Fan 160°C/Gas 4 (or light the barbecue). Place the chicken breast-side down on a chopping board, and using a pair of kitchen scissors, cut down either side of the backbone (push the thighs out of their joints as you do this so you can cut through easily) and pull the backbone out. Make sure the 'oysters' (the little nubs of flesh located where the thigh meets the backbone) stay attached to the thighs. Turn the chicken over, pull the back open and press down on the breast to flatten it; you should hear a crunching sound.

Mix the paprika, chilli powder, cumin, ketchup, sugar and vinegar together with 1–2 tablespoons of olive oil and season, and rub the mix all over the chicken. Lay the chicken on a wire rack set in a roasting tin and cook for 1¼–1½ hours, or lay it on a barbecue grill in which the coals are grey, and grill, turning the chicken regularly so it doesn't burn, until it is cooked through. Remove, cover and set to one side to rest.

Meanwhile, butter a 20cm square baking tin. Melt 50g of the butter in a pan, remove from the heat and whisk in the buttermilk, milk and eggs. Put the polenta, flour, sugar and baking powder in a bowl with a good pinch of salt and stir in the buttermilk mixture.

Spoon the cornbread mixture into the prepared tin, level, and bake for 20 minutes, or until the sides are brown and the top feels firm. Dot with the remaining butter and cut into squares. Serve warm with the chicken.

Per serving 966 kcal, **protein** 52g, **carbohydrate** 97.7g, **fat** 41.2g, **saturated fat** 16.4g, **fibre** 2.1g, **salt** 1.9g

Roast chicken with garlic, thyme croutons and salsa verde

1 hour 40 minutes | serves 4 | easy

1 whole chicken
 (about 1.5kg)
olive oil
½ day-old sourdough loaf,
 cut into large chunks
few sprigs of thyme
1 whole bulb garlic, halved
1 lemon, halved
salt and freshly ground
 black pepper

For the salsa verde
½ tbsp Dijon mustard
2 tbsp red wine vinegar
100ml olive oil
2 tbsp finely diced gherkins
2 tbsp small capers, rinsed
 and drained
1 garlic clove, crushed
½ small bunch of flat-leaf
 parsley, leaves finely
 chopped
½ small bunch of mint,
 leaves finely chopped
small bunch of basil, leaves
 finely chopped

Everyone loves a Sunday roast, and this roast chicken with garlic and thyme croutons makes it even better. Big chunky pieces of sourdough form a trivet for the roast chicken and soak up all the delicious juices while it cooks.

Preheat the oven to 200°C/Fan 180°C/Gas 6. Rub the chicken with olive oil and season well.

Toss the bread with the thyme, 2 tablespoons of olive oil and some seasoning. Spread the chunks out in the bottom of a sturdy, non-stick roasting tin with the garlic and lemon, then sit the chicken on top, keeping lots of the bread under the chicken. Roast for 1 hour 15 minutes, or until the chicken is cooked and the bread is crisp and dark golden.

To make the salsa verde, whisk the mustard and vinegar with the oil in a bowl and season well. Stir in the remaining ingredients.

Take the chicken out of the oven and leave it to rest, covered loosely with foil, then carve. Toss the croutons with all the juices from the roasting tin, then serve with the chicken and salsa verde.

Per serving 806 kcals, **protein** 52.8g, **carbohydrate** 27.2g, **fat** 53.5g, **saturated fat** 10.7g, **fibre** 2.2g, **salt** 1.5g

Roast chicken with morels

1 hour 45 minutes | serves 4 | easy

20g dried porcini
 mushrooms
1 whole chicken
 (about 1.5kg)
100g butter, at room
 temperature
100ml water
vegetable oil
2 small shallots, finely
 diced
splash of brandy
handful of fresh morels
 (or dried morels, soaked
 then drained)
200g crème fraîche
small bunch of parsley,
 leaves roughly chopped
small bunch of tarragon,
 leaves roughly chopped
salt and freshly ground
 black pepper

Morels are a type of mushroom that appear in the shops in spring during March and April – their earthy, rich flavour makes a roast chicken really special.

Preheat the oven to 200°C/Fan 180°C/Gas 6 and soak half the porcini in a small heatproof bowl of just-boiled water for 10 minutes.

Put the butter in a small bowl. Drain the porcini, pat them dry on kitchen paper, then roughly chop and add them to the butter. Season well and mix. Put the porcini butter inside the cavity of the bird and put the bird in a roasting tin. Pour the water into the cavity (this will help steam the bird from the inside). Rub the chicken all over with vegetable oil, then season. Put the bird in the oven and roast for 1 hour 15 minutes.

Grind the remaining dried porcini to a powder in either a pestle and mortar or a spice grinder.

Check the bird after the cooking time by piercing the fat part of the thigh with a skewer – the juices should run clear (if they don't, give it an extra 10–15 minutes in the oven). Gently lift the bird from the roasting tin (keeping the porcini butter inside) and leave to rest, covered loosely in foil, until you're ready to serve.

Remove half the fat from the roasting tin. Put the tin over a low heat, add the shallots and cook gently – there should be enough fat in the tin to cook the shallots, and all the scrapings will add loads of flavour. Add the dried porcini powder and cook for 2 minutes to release the aroma. Add the brandy and flambé. Keep a pan lid to hand in case you need to dampen the flames. When the flames die down, add the morels and stir, then tip in all the juices, butter and porcini from the resting chicken and bring to a simmer. Cook for a few minutes, add the crème fraîche and mix well. Stir in the fresh herbs. Serve the chicken with the sauce.

Per serving 804 kcals, **protein** 50.4g, **carbohydrate** 4.2g, **fat** 64.3g, **saturated fat** 33.5g, **fibre** 1.7g, **salt** 0.86g

Slow-roast chicken

2½ hours | serves 4 | easy

1 whole chicken
  (about 1.5kg)
1 onion, cut into fat slices
1 lemon, quartered
3 sprigs of thyme,
  rosemary and parsley
  (1 of each)
2 bay leaves
2 garlic cloves, lightly
  smashed
knob of butter
glass of white wine
  (about 175ml)
olive oil
1kg small charlotte
  potatoes, halved
  lengthways
100ml chicken stock
salt and freshly ground
  black pepper

Perfect for a lazy Sunday lunch, the juices from the chicken roast the potatoes perfectly.

Preheat the oven to 160°C/Fan 140°C/Gas 3. Trim any excess fat and skin off the chicken. Lay two slices of onion in a roasting tin, stuff the rest into the chicken along with the lemon, herbs and garlic. Loosen the skin on the breast of the chicken with your hand and push the butter under the skin. Put the chicken on top of the onion rings in the tin and pour the wine into the cavity.

Season the skin. Add a generous slug of olive oil to the tin and tip in the potatoes, season and turn them to make sure they are well coated, add the stock to the tin. Cover with foil and cook the chicken for 1 hour 30 minutes.

Turn the oven temperature up to 200°C/Fan 180°C/Gas 6. Remove the foil, turn the potatoes over and cook for a further 30–40 minutes, or until the skin is crisp and the potatoes browned.

Per serving 656 kcals, **protein** 51.8g, **carbohydrate** 43.3g, **fat** 30.3g, **saturated fat** 10.4g, **fibre** 2.7g, **salt** 0.72g

From afar

Butter chicken curry

45 minutes | serves 2 | easy

2 tbsp butter
1 large onion, thinly sliced
4 skinless chicken thigh
  fillets, cut into bite-sized
  pieces
4cm piece of fresh root
  ginger, peeled and grated
2 garlic cloves, crushed
2 tbsp makhani or other
  mild curry paste
1 tbsp ground almonds
  (optional)
6 tbsp Greek yoghurt
100ml chicken stock
handful of coriander leaves
salt and freshly ground
  black pepper
basmati rice, to serve
naan bread, to serve

Ground almonds add extra richness to this classic masala, so do add them if you have some in your store cupboard; it is still very good without them though.

Melt the butter in a large, wide saucepan and cook the onion for 5 minutes, until soft. Add the chicken and cook for 5 minutes, stirring, until starting to brown.

Mix the ginger, garlic, curry paste, almonds (if using) and yoghurt in a bowl then stir them into the pan with the chicken and cook for 2–3 minutes. Add the stock, season and bring to a simmer. Reduce the heat and simmer gently for 20 minutes. Scatter over coriander leaves and serve with basmati rice and naan bread.

Per serving 449 kcals, **protein** 42.4g, **carbohydrate** 12.9g, **fat** 25.3g, **saturated fat** 12.3g, **fibre** 2.7g, **salt** 1.4g

Chettinad chicken

30 minutes, plus marinating | serves 6 | easy

3 garlic cloves, peeled

4cm piece of fresh root
  ginger, peeled

750g boneless, skinless
  chicken thigh fillets,
  quartered

1 tsp ground turmeric

3 tbsp vegetable oil

2 onions, sliced

2 thumb-sized red chillies,
  deseeded and sliced

1 tbsp tomato purée

3 tbsp desiccated coconut,
  toasted

2 cinnamon sticks

350ml vegetable stock

salt and freshly ground
  black pepper

For the spice mix

1½ tsp each of fennel
  seeds, cumin seeds
  and coriander seeds

1 dried long red chilli

1 star anise

A fiery curry from Southern India: the marinating takes time, but the recipe is quick to prepare and cook. Friends who are fans of hot chicken curries will love this. Serve with rice or naan bread alongside.

Toast the spices for the spice mix in a small dry frying pan until fragrant, then grind them in a spice grinder or pestle and mortar and set aside.

Purée the garlic and ginger in a blender with a little water. Put the chicken in a bowl with the turmeric and garlic/ginger paste, and grind over some black pepper. Leave to marinate, covered, for 30 minutes or overnight in the fridge.

Heat the vegetable oil and add the onions and red chilli. Season with salt and fry for 10 minutes until soft. Add the marinated chicken, toasted spices, tomato purée, toasted desiccated coconut and cinnamon sticks, and fry for 5 minutes. Pour in the stock and simmer for 30 minutes. Serve with basmati rice or naan bread.

Per serving 268 kcals, protein 27.5g, carbohdyrate 5.6g, fat 14.2g, saturated fat 5.7g, fibre 3.2g, salt 0.5g

Chicken pasanda

50 minutes, plus marinating | serves 2 | easy

4 skinless chicken thigh
  fillets, quartered
4 tbsp natural yoghurt
1 tsp ground cumin
2 tsp ground coriander
4 cardamom pods, split
  and seeds crushed
1 tsp ground turmeric
1 tbsp oil, for frying
1 onion, finely sliced
2cm piece of fresh root
  ginger, grated
1 green chilli, sliced, plus
  extra to serve (optional)
1 garlic clove, crushed
100ml chicken stock
2 tbsp ground almonds
1 tsp garam masala
salt and freshly ground
  black pepper
yoghurt, to serve

This is a mild curry, with a creamy but light sauce made from yoghurt and almonds. Serve with a side of basmati rice.

Put the chicken, yoghurt and spices in a bowl. Mix to coat the chicken and marinate for at least 1–2 hours.

Heat the oil in a saucepan and cook the onion for about 10 minutes until soft and golden. Add the grated ginger, chilli and garlic and cook for a further few minutes until fragrant. Tip in the chicken and marinade then cook, stirring, until the chicken starts to colour. Add the stock, season, cover and simmer for 30 minutes.

Stir 4–5 tablespoons of the cooking liquid into the ground almonds then add everything back to the pan. Add the garam masala and simmer for 5 minutes. Serve with yoghurt and some thinly sliced green chilli if you like.

Per serving 575 kcals, protein 54.3g, carbohydrate 15.9g, fat 33.3g, saturated fat 6.4g, fibre 2.7g, salt 0.9g

Chicken dhansak with spiced garlic naan

1 hour 15 minutes | serves 4 | easy

100g red lentils
2 onions, roughly chopped
400g can chopped
  tomatoes
1 tsp ground turmeric
1 tsp salt
1 tsp cumin seeds
1 tsp coriander seeds
4 cardamom pods, split
  and seeds crushed
1 tbsp oil
4cm piece of fresh root
  ginger, peeled and finely
  grated
3 garlic cloves, crushed
2–3 green chillies, sliced
  (deseeded if you like)
6 skinless, boneless
  chicken thighs, quartered
150ml water
1 tsp garam masala, plus
  extra for sprinkling
small bunch of coriander,
  leaves chopped
knob of butter
4 mini naan breads

Chicken and lentils cooked in a spicy Indian tomato sauce makes this dhansak, a popular Indian meal, a filling and warming supper. Serve with garlic naan breads on the side.

Put the lentils, onions and tomatoes in a pan with the turmeric and salt. Add water to just cover, then simmer gently for about 20 minutes, or until the lentils are very tender. Remove from the heat and set aside.

Meanwhile, toast the whole spices in a dry frying pan until fragrant. Grind them in a pestle and mortar or spice grinder.

Heat the oil in a large non-stick frying pan, add the ginger, all but 1 teaspoon of the garlic, most of the chilli and the toasted spices then cook gently for 2–3 minutes. Add the chicken and cook, stirring, until opaque, then tip in the cooked lentils and the water. Simmer for 45 minutes, then stir in the garam masala and sprinkle with coriander.

Melt the butter in a small frying pan and fry the reserved garlic, green chilli and another pinch of garam masala. Brush the naans with the butter, then heat them through in a hot oven and serve with the curry.

Per serving 501 kcals, **protein** 40.2g, **carbohydrate** 52g, **fat** 13.4g, **saturated fat** 2.4g, **fibre** 6.2g, **salt** 2.2g

Chicken and butternut squash curry with cumin and coriander rice

1½ hours | serves 4 | easy

2 tbsp vegetable oil
2 onions, finely chopped
1 red chilli, finely sliced
  (deseeded if you like)
4cm piece of fresh root
  ginger, peeled and finely
  chopped
1 tbsp ground coriander
1 tbsp ground turmeric
1 tbsp medium curry
  powder
8 skinless, boneless
  chicken thighs, quartered
400ml can coconut milk
400ml chicken stock
400g butternut squash,
  peeled and cut into
  chunks
½ small bunch of coriander,
  leaves chopped
salt and freshly ground
  black pepper

An easy chicken curry that beats a takeaway any day. With butternut squash and fresh coriander as well as Indian spices, it's sure to be a dinner table favourite.

Heat the oil in a deep frying pan or casserole, add the onions and fry until soft and golden. Stir in the chilli, ginger and spices for a minute, followed by the chicken, coconut milk and stock. Season. Bring to a simmer, then cover and cook for 30 minutes.

Remove the lid, stir in the squash and simmer for a further 15–20 minutes, until both squash and chicken are tender and the sauce is reduced to a nice consistency.

Meanwhile, cook the rice until tender and drain well. Toast the cumin seeds in a small, dry frying pan for a couple of minutes until fragrant. Stir the cumin seeds and chopped coriander through the warm rice. Stir the rest of the coriander into the curry and serve with the cumin and coriander rice.

Per serving 770 kcals, **protein** 48.3g, **carbohydrate** 74.9g, **fat** 29.8g, **saturated fat** 17.3g, **fibre** 5g, **salt** 0.7g

Chicken bhuna

40 minutes | serves 4 | easy

1 tbsp sunflower oil
2 medium onions, halved
and finely sliced
4 garlic cloves, finely
chopped
25g piece of fresh root
ginger, peeled and finely
chopped
2 green chillies, finely
chopped (deseeded if
you like)
2 heaped tsp cardamom
pods, seeds crushed
2 tsp ground cumin
2 tsp ground coriander
1 tsp fennel seeds
juice of ½ lemon
4 skinless chicken breasts,
cut into bite-sized pieces
400g can of chopped
tomatoes
150ml water
pinch of salt
pinch of sugar
basmati rice, to serve

A classic Indian dish, this recipe is easy to make and will satisfy your takeaway cravings.

Heat the oil in a large non-stick frying pan and cook the onion until soft and lightly coloured. Add the garlic, ginger and chilli and cook for a further 2 minutes. Sprinkle in the spices and fry for another minute.

Stir in the lemon juice and chicken and cook for 2 minutes. Pour the tomatoes into the pan, add the water, salt and sugar and bring to a simmer. Cook for 15 minutes, stirring occasionally. Remove from the heat and serve with steamed basmati rice.

Per serving 240 kcals, **protein** 36.9g, **carbohydrate** 11g, **fat** 5.6g, **saturated fat** 0.9g, **fibre** 1.9g, **salt** 0.36g

West Indian chicken curry

30 minutes | serves 4 | easy

1 tsp oil
1 large onion, chopped
2 garlic cloves, chopped
2 tbsp curry powder
1 large sweet potato,
   peeled and cut into
   small chunks
4 skinless chicken breasts,
   cut into bite-sized pieces
400ml can of coconut milk
100g whole cherry
   tomatoes
salt and freshly ground
   black pepper
fresh coriander leaves,
   to serve
basmati rice, to serve

This fragrant, homemade curry with coconut and sweet potato is ready for the table in just half an hour, and makes a filling mid-week dish for four.

Heat the oil in a large non-stick frying pan and cook the onion and garlic for 5 minutes, until soft and lightly coloured. Season, then stir in the curry powder. Cook for a further minute, then add the sweet potato and chicken.

Pour in the coconut milk. Simmer for 10–12 minutes, then add the tomatoes and simmer for 2 minutes. Serve sprinkled with fresh coriander and a side of steamed basmati rice.

Per serving 417 kcals, protein 37.6g, carbohydrate 25.6g, fat 19g, saturated fat 14.5g, fibre 4.6g, salt 0.67g

Chicken tikka

1 hour, plus marinating | serves 4 | easy

2 garlic cloves, crushed

40g piece of fresh root ginger, peeled and grated

small bunch of coriander, leaves finely chopped

100g Greek yoghurt

powdered beetroot or other red colouring (optional)

1 tsp salt, plus extra to season

8 chicken thighs (bone in and skin removed and discarded)

2 lemons, 1 juiced and 1 cut into wedges

For the tandoori spice

1 tsp black peppercorns

½ tsp cumin seeds, toasted

1 tsp coriander seeds, toasted

5cm piece of cinnamon stick

1 tsp cayenne pepper

You can colour your chicken as red as you like, or leave out the colouring for a more natural look. Skewer these thighs with the bone in for a better shape (and keeping the bone in means you can eat them with your fingers). Serve on a bed of freshly chopped salad with a side of Greek yoghurt.

Start by grinding all the tandoori spices together in a pestle and mortar or spice grinder. Put them into a large bowl with the garlic, ginger, coriander, yoghurt, red colouring, if using, and the salt then mix well. Make three deep cuts into each thigh with a sharp knife. Pour over the lemon juice and toss, then add the chicken thighs to the yoghurt mix and turn them over in the mixture. Leave to marinate for a couple of hours or overnight.

Push the thighs onto long metal skewers, three on each, pushing a skewer through each side under the bone. Sprinkle with salt. Heat the oven to 220°C/Fan 200°C/Gas 7. Put the skewers onto a rack set over a roasting tin and cook for 40–50 minutes, until they are cooked through and starting to turn a very dark brown at the edges, turning them over once or twice. Serve with the lemon wedges and salad.

Per serving 339 kcals, **protein** 29.1g, **carbohydrate** 4.1g, **fat** 23.3g, **saturated fat** 7.3g, **fibre** 0.1g, **salt** 1.5g

Indian-spiced roast chicken

2 hours | serves 4 | easy

4cm piece of fresh root
  ginger, finely grated
2 garlic cloves, crushed
1 green chilli, finely
  chopped (deseeded
  if you like)
2 tsp ground cumin
2 tsp ground coriander
1 tsp ground turmeric
1 tbsp groundnut oil
1 whole chicken (about
  1.5kg)
165ml can of coconut milk
salt and freshly ground
  black pepper

For the lemon rice
2 tbsp oil
strips of rind from
  1 lemon
1 tsp mustard seeds
2 cardamom pods, bruised
300g basmati rice
light chicken stock

If you're feeling bored of your usual Sunday roast chicken, give this spiced version a go. Buying a whole chicken often offers better value than buying breast fillets, plus any leftovers can be eaten with salad the next day.

Preheat the oven to 190°C/Fan 170°C/Gas 5. Mix the ginger, garlic, chilli and spices with the groundnut oil and rub the mix all over the chicken. Put the chicken in a baking tin, season and roast for 1 hour. Pour over the coconut milk, then continue cooking for a further 30 minutes.

While the chicken is roasting, make the lemon rice. Heat the oil in a saucepan. Add the lemon rind strips, mustard seeds and cardamom pods, and leave to sizzle and pop for 2 minutes. Tip in the rice and stir to coat. Add the stock and bring to a boil, then turn the heat down to a low heat, cover and leave to simmer for 12–15 minutes until the rice is tender and the liquid has been absorbed (add a splash of water if you need to). Season and serve with the chicken.

Per serving 933 kcals, **protein** 57.1g, **carbohydrate** 58.5g, **fat** 50.6g, **saturated fat** 17.4g, **fibre** 0.9g, **salt** 0.7g

Chinese red-braised chicken

30 minutes | serves 4 | easy

1 tbsp oil, for frying
8 small chicken thighs
  (leave the bone in and
  pull the skin off)
4cm piece of fresh root
  ginger, peeled and
  shredded
2 garlic cloves, finely sliced
1 star anise
4 spring onions, sliced,
  plus extra to serve
100ml Chinese rice wine
  or dry sherry
2 tbsp soy sauce
50g brown sugar
150ml water
1 head of broccoli, cut into
  florets
sesame oil, for drizzling
steamed rice, to serve
1 red chilli, deseeded and
  shredded, to serve

This Chinese-inspired chicken dish is quick, easy and comes in at under 400 calories!

Heat the oil in a large frying pan, add the chicken and cook for 5 minutes, turning, until lightly golden. Add the ginger, garlic, star anise and spring onions. Cook for a minute then add the rice wine or sherry, soy sauce, brown sugar and water. Reduce the heat, simmer and cook, covered, for 20 minutes, turning the chicken every now and again.

Uncover, then continue to cook until the sauce has reduced and is glazing the chicken. Cook the broccoli florets then toss with a little drizzle of sesame oil.

Serve the chicken in bowls with steamed rice, the broccoli and the sauce spooned over. Scatter over chilli and extra sliced spring onion to serve.

Per serving 359 kcals, **protein** 40.5g, **carbohydrate** 20g, **fat** 9g, **saturated fat** 1.9g, **fibre** 4.3g, **salt** 1.9g

Peking-style chicken with spring onion stir-fry

45 minutes | serves 2 | easy

4 whole chicken thighs
  (bone in, skin on)
2 tsp Chinese five-spice
2 tsp runny honey
1 tsp soy sauce
groundnut oil, for
  stir-frying
½ small head of Chinese
  leaf, shredded
6 spring onions, sliced
small piece of fresh root
  ginger, peeled and cut
  into matchsticks
1 red chilli, shredded
  (deseeded if you like)
salt and freshly ground
  black pepper
sesame oil, to finish
  (optional)

**Peking-style means this chicken is equal parts sweet and spicy.
You can serve it with a small side of rice, if you like.**

Heat the oven to 200°C/Fan 180°C/Gas 6. Put the chicken thighs on a
baking tray skin-side up and bake for 30 minutes. Mix the five-spice,
honey and soy sauce in a bowl.

Remove the chicken from the oven and drain away any excess fat, then brush
the thighs all over with the five-spice mix and cook for a further 15 minutes.

Heat a little oil in a wok or frying pan and stir-fry the Chinese leaf and
spring onions, ginger and chilli for a couple of minutes (keep it nice and
crisp). Season. Finish with a little sesame oil, if using.

Per serving 482 kcals, **protein** 41.3g, **carbohydrate** 7.2g, **fat** 32.3g, **saturated fat** 8.7g, **fibre** 0.7g, **salt** 0.8g

Sticky lemon and chilli chicken noodles

20 minutes | serves 2 | easy

100g thread egg noodles
2 skinless chicken breasts,
    cut into strips
1 tsp cornflour
1 tbsp oil
4 spring onions, halved
    and sliced into lengths
50g mangetout, sliced
1 red pepper, deseeded
    and sliced
2 tbsp soy sauce
juice of 1 lemon
1 tbsp runny honey
2 tbsp chilli sauce
salt and freshly ground
    black pepper

Recreate a Chinese takeaway at home with this healthy chicken noodle dish, served in a sweet and spicy lemon, chilli and honey sauce. The bonus of making it yourself is knowing exactly what's in it!

Cook the noodles according to the packet instructions, then drain and set aside.

Toss the chicken with the cornflour and some seasoning. Heat the oil in a non-stick wok or large frying pan and stir-fry the chicken until golden. Scoop the chicken out and transfer it to a plate, then add the veg to the pan, keeping back some spring onion, and toss over a high heat for a couple of minutes.

Return the chicken to the pan with the soy sauce, lemon, honey and chilli sauce, add a splash of water and let it bubble away for a few minutes. Check that the chicken is cooked through then remove from the heat and toss with the noodles. Sprinkle over the remaining spring onion to serve.

Per serving 477 kcals, **protein** 42.3g, **carbohydrate** 54.1g, **fat** 11.7g, **saturated fat** 1.4g, **fibre** 3.6g, **salt** 4.17g

Chicken and sweetcorn dumpling soup

40 minutes | serves 4 | easy

2 egg noodle nests
200g skinless chicken
  breast fillets, finely
  chopped
4 spring onions, 2 finely
  chopped, 2 sliced
2 tsp peeled and grated
  ginger
1 corn on the cob, kernels
  sliced off
3 tbsp soy sauce
20 wonton wrappers
1 litre chicken stock
salt and freshly ground
  black pepper
chilli oil, to serve (optional)

An easy-to-follow recipe for chicken soup at its heartwarming best. With noodles and wonton dumplings, this Asian-flavoured broth is both light and filling.

Cook the noodles according to the packet instructions, then drain and set aside.

Mix the chicken with the chopped spring onion and half of the grated ginger in a bowl. Cook 3 tablespoons of the sweetcorn kernels in simmering water for 2 minutes, then drain and add them to the chicken with 1 tablespoon of soy sauce and season. Use this mix to fill the wonton wrappers, wetting the edges so you can pinch them together into a triangle shape.

Bring the chicken stock to a simmer and add the sliced spring onions, remaining corn, ginger, and soy sauce. Add the wontons and cook them for 5 minutes, until the chicken is cooked through. Stir in the noodles to heat them through. Add a drop of chilli oil to each bowl of soup to serve, if you like.

Per serving 355 kcals, **protein** 29.1g, **carbohydrate** 51.9g, **fat** 2.6g, **saturated fat** 0.7g, **fibre** 3.5g, **salt** 3.9g

Sesame miso chicken with sweet and sour salad

30 minutes | serves 2 | easy

1 tbsp miso paste

1 tbsp soy sauce

4 tsp golden caster sugar

2 tsp sesame oil

2 tbsp rice vinegar

4 skinless chicken thigh fillets, halved

2 carrots, peeled and cut into thin batons

½ cucumber, seeds scraped out and cut into strips

10 radishes, finely sliced

250g cooked brown basmati rice

2 spring onions, thinly sliced, to garnish

Miso paste is a great ingredient to have to hand: it keeps for ages in the fridge and adds a wonderful deep, savoury flavour to Asian soups and marinades.

Mix the miso paste, soy sauce, 2 teaspoons of the sugar, 1 teaspoon of the sesame oil and 1 tablespoon of the vinegar in a bowl and toss with the chicken. Leave for 15 minutes.

Heat the remaining sugar and vinegar until dissolved, cool, then toss with the veg.

Heat the grill to hot. Cook the chicken for about 10 minutes, turning it regularly, until sticky, glazed, and cooked through. Toss the cooked rice with the rest of the sesame oil then serve with the chicken and salad, and garnish with spring onions.

Per serving 478 kcals, **protein** 42.5g, **carbohydrate** 52.1g, **fat** 12.5g, **saturated fat** 2.4g, **fibre** 6.2g, **salt** 3.57g

Japanese chicken curry

30 minutes | serves 4 | easy

2 tbsp vegetable oil

500g skinless, boneless
   chicken thighs, halved

1 onion, chopped

2 garlic cloves, chopped

1 tbsp peeled and grated
   ginger

1 tbsp miso paste

1 tbsp mild curry powder

400ml chicken stock

100g green beans,
   trimmed

salt and freshly ground
   black pepper

steamed rice, to serve

Adding miso paste gives this curry a distinct Japanese taste. You can find the intense savoury paste in health food shops and Asian supermarkets.

Heat 1 tablespoon of oil in a non-stick frying pan and brown the chicken pieces on both sides until golden. Remove the chicken from the pan and add the onion, garlic, ginger and the remaining oil. Cook for 5 minutes.

Add the miso paste, curry powder, stock and season, and return the browned chicken to the pan. Bring to a boil then turn down to a simmer and cook over a medium heat for 20 minutes, adding the beans for the last 5 minutes. Serve with steamed rice.

Per serving 203 kcals, **protein** 28.2g, **carbohydrate** 6.1g, **fat** 7.5g, **saturated fat** 1.7g, **fibre** 1.8g, **salt** 1.43g

Yakitori chicken skewers with carrot 'slaw

45 minutes | serves 2 | easy

3 carrots, grated

¼ mooli, grated (or handful of finely sliced radishes)

5 spring onions, 4 cut into 3cm lengths, 1 thinly sliced

small piece of fresh root ginger, peeled and grated

1 red chilli, thinly sliced (deseeded if you like)

2 tsp sesame oil

juice of 1 lime

1½ tbsp rice wine vinegar

4 tbsp soy sauce

2 tbsp mirin

2 tbsp chicken stock

1 tbsp golden caster sugar

4 skinless, boneless chicken thighs, quartered

A Japanese mirin glaze is ideal for grilled meat, poultry or fish; it is so easy to make, and it makes these healthy chicken skewers deliciously sticky.

Put the carrot, mooli, sliced spring onions, ginger and red chilli in a bowl. Add the sesame oil and lime juice, toss together and set aside.

Put the rice wine vinegar, soy sauce, mirin, stock and sugar in a small saucepan and simmer for 5 minutes. Cool, then toss with the chicken and leave for 15 minutes. Preheat the grill.

Thread the chicken pieces onto 4 metal skewers, adding a piece of spring onion in between each chunk.

Grill or barbecue the chicken, brushing it with the remaining marinade, until cooked through and glazed. Serve with the 'slaw.

Per serving 440 kcals, **protein** 33.8g, **carbohydrate** 33.5g, **fat** 17.4g, **saturated fat** 4.3g, **fibre** 5.4g, **salt** 6.0g

Sesame chicken, pickled red cabbage and sushi rice salad

45 minutes | serves 2 | easy

4 tbsp rice wine vinegar

3 tbsp golden caster sugar

1 large carrot, shredded

1 small red cabbage, cored
and shredded

chicken stock

1 large skinless chicken
breast fillet

100g sushi rice

150ml water

100g soya beans, blanched
and cooled

sesame oil, to drizzle

salt and freshly ground
black pepper

toasted black or white
sesame seeds, for
sprinkling (optional)

If you love sushi but have never made it at home, try this easy salad version first. We've made it with pickled red cabbage, sesame chicken, soya beans and sushi rice.

Heat the vinegar and sugar in a small pan until the sugar dissolves. Keep 3 tablespoons of the vinegar and sugar mix back, then put the carrot and cabbage in separate bowls and divide the rest of the vinegar mix between them. Toss in the mix and set aside until you are ready to serve.

Heat a small saucepan with enough chicken stock to cover the chicken breast. When it simmers, add the chicken and poach it gently for 10–12 minutes, or until it is cooked through, remove to cool then slice the chicken.

Wash the sushi rice in water, then drain and repeat a couple of times to get rid of some starch. Put it in a saucepan with the water. Bring to the boil, then cover and lower the heat. Cook for 12–15 minutes until the water is absorbed, then tip it onto a plate to cool. Sprinkle over the reserved vinegar mix.

Arrange the rice on plates with the pickled veg and beans. Add the chicken, season and sprinkle over a little drizzle of sesame oil and some toasted sesame seeds, if you like.

Per serving 515 kcals, **protein** 31.4g, **carbohydrate** 79.9g, **fat** 5.8g, **saturated fat** 0.9g, **fibre** 8.8g, **salt** 0.4g

Bang bang chicken

45 minutes | serves 4 | easy

6 skinless chicken thigh
  fillets
400ml can of coconut milk
1 tbsp fish sauce
4 spring onions, finely
  sliced and cut into 5cm
  lengths
½ cucumber, seeds scraped
  out and flesh grated
300g fine green beans,
  trimmed, blanched and
  split lengthways
1 tbsp rice vinegar
1 red chilli, finely grated

For the peanut sauce

2 tsp sesame seeds, lightly
  toasted
125g smooth peanut
  butter
100ml boiling water
2 red chillies, deseeded
  and finely diced
3 tbsp soy sauce
2 tbsp sesame oil

Spicy and sweet, this chicken recipe can be served as a main with rice or as a light starter salad.

Put the chicken fillets in a wide, shallow pan with the coconut milk and fish sauce, bring to the boil, then reduce the heat and simmer, covered, for 10 minutes. Take the chicken off the heat and leave to cool completely in the sauce.

To make the peanut sauce, pound half the toasted sesame seeds in a pestle and mortar. Put the peanut butter and crushed sesame seeds in a saucepan with the boiling water and warm gently for 5 minutes, stirring occasionally. Stir in the chillies and the soy sauce then remove the pan from the heat and whisk in the oil gradually, until the sauce can be poured easily. You might need to add a little more boiling water to loosen it to pouring consistency.

Remove the chicken from the coconut milk and shred. Spoon some peanut sauce onto plates then layer the chicken and vegetables and sprinkle over the remaining sesame seeds, rice vinegar and shredded chilli.

Per serving 594 kcals, **protein** 34.7g, **carbohydrate** 13.5g, **fat** 44.2g, **saturated fat** 21g, **fibre** 3.4g, **salt** 3.3g

Thai chicken, cucumber and coconut salad

30 minutes | serves 4 | easy

400g skinless chicken
  thigh fillets
165ml can of coconut milk
40g palm sugar (or
  demerara sugar)
3 tbsp fish sauce
1 large cucumber, cut into
  long, thin ribbons with a
  vegetable peeler
2 long red chillies, thinly
  sliced (deseeded if you
  like)
small bunch of coriander,
  leaves picked
1 Thai shallot or regular
  shallot, finely sliced
50g roasted peanuts,
  crushed

Cucumber gives a fresh, crisp base to this salad, and poaching the chicken in coconut milk makes the meat really tender.

Put the chicken fillets between two sheets of cling film and bash them with a meat hammer or rolling pin to flatten them a little (try to flatten them each to the same thickness).

Put the coconut milk, palm sugar and fish sauce in a wide, shallow pan. Add the flattened chicken fillets then gently bring to a simmer. Cook for 15 minutes, remove from the heat and leave to cool in the liquid.

Remove the chicken from the poaching liquid and slice it as thinly as possible, then mix all of the ingredients together in a bowl, except the roasted peanuts. Serve drizzled with some of the poaching liquid and sprinkle with the crushed peanuts.

Per serving 288 kcals, **protein** 27g, **carbohydrate** 15.5g, **fat** 13.5g, **saturated fat** 5.8g, **fibre** 1.3g, **salt** 2.52g

Quick Thai jungle curry

20 minutes | serves 2 | easy

2 tbsp jungle curry paste
300ml chicken stock
small bunch of coriander,
    stalks finely chopped,
    leaves left whole
300g skinless chicken thigh
    fillets, sliced
150g mixed packet of baby
    corn and sugar snap peas
fish sauce, to taste
1 tsp brown sugar
1 lime, ½ juiced, ½ cut into
    wedges
steamed basmati rice,
    to serve

If you like hot Thai red curry, try this jungle curry – it's not as rich as it contains no coconut milk, but beware, it is fiery.

Heat a non-stick saucepan and put in the curry paste and a splash of the stock. Fry for a few minutes, until you can smell all of the aromatics from the paste. Add the remaining stock and coriander stalks and simmer for 2–3 minutes.

Add the chicken and simmer until the chicken is cooked through. Add the veg and cook for a couple of minutes until just tender. Stir in a good splash of fish sauce, the sugar and the lime juice and cook for 30 seconds. Serve with steamed rice, a scattering of the coriander leaves and lime wedges to squeeze over.

Per serving 254 kcals, protein 38.9g, carbohydrate 7g, fat 8g, saturated fat 1.4g, fibre 3.1g, salt 1.8g

African chicken, sweet potato and peanut curry

1½ hours | serves 4 | easy

150g smooth peanut butter

2 onions, 1 roughly
   chopped, 1 diced

50g peeled fresh root ginger

1 tbsp ground cumin

2 tsp ground coriander

1 tsp ground turmeric

1 tsp cayenne pepper

1 scotch bonnet chilli,
   halved lengthways and
   deseeded

1 tsp vegetable oil

½ tsp ground white or
   black pepper

400g can coconut milk

1 chicken stock cube,
   crumbled

8 chicken thighs, skinned

500g sweet potatoes,
   peeled, halved lengthways
   and cut into chunks

salt and freshly ground
   black pepper

To serve

good handful of coriander

1 red chilli, deseeded and
   finely sliced

2 tbsp roasted peanuts,
   roughly chopped

cooked rice

a few lime wedges

This African curry makes for a delicious family meal. It also freezes well: cool the curry, then transfer it to freezer containers or food bags to freeze completely. The night before eating, defrost the curry in the fridge overnight and cook as below.

Put the peanut butter into a heatproof bowl, add 400ml boiling water and mix until smooth.

Put the roughly chopped onion, ginger, spices and scotch bonnet chilli into a food processor or blender, and blitz to a smooth paste – if it's too dry, add some of the peanut water.

Heat the oil in a large saucepan, add the diced onion and fry until soft. Stir in the spice paste with the white or black pepper and fry for a few minutes more until fragrant. Add the coconut milk and peanut water, followed by the chicken stock cube and chicken thighs. Cover and simmer for 45 minutes, stirring occasionally so nothing sticks to the bottom of the pan.

Add the sweet potato and cook, uncovered, for 15 minutes if freezing or 20 minutes if eating straight away. If the sauce is too thick, add a splash of water. Season well.

To serve, scatter the coriander leaves, fresh chilli and chopped peanuts over the top. Serve with rice and lime wedges.

Per serving 770 kcals, **protein** 49.7g, **carbohydrate** 39.5g, **fat** 44.6g, **saturated fat** 21.6g, **fibre** 5.8g, **salt** 1.6g

Moroccan wings with herb couscous

30 minutes | serves 4 | easy

2 x 475g packs of chicken
  wings
3 tbsp maple syrup
1 tsp harissa paste, plus
  more to serve (optional)
1 tsp cumin seeds, lightly
  crushed
grated zest and juice of
  1 lemon
grated zest and juice of
  1 medium orange (about
  6 tbsp in total)
150g couscous
large bunch of mint, leaves
  roughly chopped
large bunch of coriander,
  leaves roughly chopped
2 tbsp finely chopped
  preserved lemon
1 tbsp extra-virgin olive oil
salt and freshly ground
  black pepper
0% fat Greek yoghurt,
  to serve

**A spicy, citrusy dish that is complemented with a fragrant couscous.
Tone down the heat with a spoonful of yoghurt.**

Heat the grill to high. Put the chicken wings into a large roasting tin and
grill for 15 minutes, turning halfway, until golden.

Meanwhile, mix the maple syrup, harissa paste and cumin with the lemon
and orange zests, half of the lemon and orange juices and some seasoning.
Pour the mixture over the wings, shake to coat them, then return them to
the grill for another 15 minutes, turning once, until the wings are browned
and sticky.

For the couscous, boil the kettle. Place the couscous in a heaproof bowl,
splash the remaining lemon and orange juice over the couscous then pour
in enough boiling water just to cover. Cover the bowl with cling film and
set aside for 10 minutes.

Fluff up the couscous with a fork, fold through the chopped herbs,
preserved lemon, olive oil and some salt and pepper. Serve with the wings
and a spoonful of yoghurt, swirled with harissa if you like a bit more heat.

Per serving 503 kcals, **protein** 37.4g, **carbohydrate** 29.8g, **fat** 25.8g, **saturated fat** 8.5g, **fibre** 0g, **salt** 0.55g

Jamaican spiced chicken with chargrilled pineapple, rice and peas

1 hour, plus marinating | serves 12 | easy

20-24 whole chicken pieces
1 medium pineapple
pinch of brown sugar
salt and freshly ground
  black pepper

For the marinade
2 scotch bonnet chillies
4 garlic cloves
1 onion, roughly chopped
2cm piece of fresh root
  ginger, peeled and sliced
1 tsp ground allspice
1 tsp nutmeg
1 tsp ground cinnamon
4 tbsp cider vinegar
juice of 1 large orange
4 tbsp soft brown sugar
2 tbsp thyme leaves, chopped
4 tbsp soy sauce
3 tbsp vegetable oil

For the rice and peas
2 bunches of spring
  onions, thinly sliced
800g basmati rice
2 x 400g tins coconut milk
1 litre vegetable stock
2 tsp ground allspice
2 x 400g tins red kidney
  beans, drained

This Caribbean-spiced meal is great for entertaining. Use whole chicken thighs and drumsticks to get the most from your chicken.

Remove the stems from the chillis and put all the marinade ingredients in a food processor and blitz until smooth. Add a good teaspoon each of salt and pepper. Cut 2-3 slashes on each piece of chicken. Put the chicken in a large bowl and toss with the marinade. Cover and chill for at least 2 hours or preferably overnight.

To make the rice and peas, shred three of the spring onions and finely chop the rest. Put all the ingredients except the beans and the shredded spring onions in a large saucepan with a tight-fitting lid. Bring to the boil then lower the heat to very low. Cover with the lid and cook for 20-25 minutes, or until the rice is just cooked. Remove the lid and remove the pan from the heat. Toss the beans through the rice and keep warm.

Heat the barbecue, and once the coals are hot, push them to one side. Cook the marinated chicken on indirect heat (not sitting directly over the coals), turning frequently, for 25-30 minutes. Peel, core and cut the pineapple into slices. In the last 5 minutes, rub the pineapple slices with oil and a little brown sugar. Grill the pineapple on both sides. Alternatively, roast the chicken in a 190°C/Fan 170°C/Gas 5 oven for 1 hour. Roast the pineapple for the last 10 minutes.

Sprinkle the chicken with the spring onions and serve with the rice and peas, and chargrilled pineapple.

Per serving 860 kcals, **protein** 38.5g, **carbohydrate** 74g, **fat** 42g, **saturated fat** 17.8g, **fibre** 4.7g, **salt** 2.1g

Caribbean chicken and black bean stew

1 hour | serves 4 | easy

olive oil, for frying
500g skinless, boneless
  chicken thighs, cut into
  bite-sized pieces
1 onion, chopped
2 garlic cloves, crushed
1 green pepper, deseeded
  and cut into chunks
1 scotch bonnet chilli,
  finely chopped
  (deseeded if you like)
2–3 tsp jerk seasoning
400g can of chopped
  tomatoes
200ml chicken stock
400g tin of black beans or
  kidney beans, drained
  and rinsed
salt and freshly ground
  black pepper
steamed basmati rice,
  to serve

This chicken recipe is full of delicious, fresh, spicy flavours. What's more is it's easy to make, low-fat and low in calories too.

Heat a little oil in a non-stick frying pan and brown the chicken all over. Remove the chicken from the pan, set aside, then add the onion, garlic, pepper and chilli and cook, stirring, until softened.

Add the jerk seasoning and cook for 1 minute. Return the chicken to the pan. Stir in the tomatoes and stock, season and bring to a simmer. Add the beans, cover and simmer gently for 40 minutes. Serve with steamed rice.

Per serving 481 kcals, **protein** 65.7g, **carbohydrate** 27g, **fat** 9.8g, **saturated fat** 2.5, **fibre** 9.4g, **salt** 1.8g

Index

Photography credits

LIGHT AND HEALTHY

Shirataki noodles with poached miso ginger chicken broth SAM STOWELL
Poached chicken with vegetable and orzo broth MYLES NEW
Spring chicken salad PETER CASSIDY
Dijon and honey glazed chicken and watercress salad MAJA SMEND
Sumac spice-crusted chicken with spiced yogurt dressing ANT DUNCAN
Herb, basmati and chicken salad MYLES NEW
Satay chicken with peanut sauce GARETH MORGANS
Chicken parmigiana light STUART OVENDEN
Chicken with agrodolce sauce GARETH MORGANS
Tamarind chicken with tomato and mint salad DAVID MUNNS
Chicken and ham pie PETER CASSIDY
Chicken with a mustard crust DAVID MUNNS
Tarragon chicken DAVID MUNNS
Chicken, leek and Dijon mustard casserole GARETH MORGANS
One-pot chicken with cannellini beans and chorizo SAM STOWELL
Sherry-braised chicken breast with horseradish crumbs DAVID MUNNS
Roast chicken with 40 cloves of garlic DAVID MUNNS

QUICK AND EASY

Chicken, pea and pasta broth SIMON WALTON
Chicken broth with orecchiette, pancetta and peas JON WHITAKER
One-pot chicken with orzo and dill LARA HOLMES
Smoky chicken, sweetcorn and pancetta salad DAVID MUNNS
Throw-it-together chicken salad PETER CASSIDY
Griddled chicken salad with basil mayo MYLES NEW
Chargrilled chicken with white beans and cabbage SAM STOWELL
Harissa chicken patties with quinoa salad DAVID MUNNS
Chicken liver, hazelnut, pancetta and apple salad MAJA SMEND
Chicken skewers with bulgar wheat and corn salad DAVID MUNNS
Italian chicken and basil burgers with tomato relish DAN JONES
Chicken and slaw baguette with hazelnut dressing PHILIP WEBB
Coconut chicken and rice one-pot DAN JONES
Mango chicken with couscous SIMON WALTON
Tagliatelle with roast chicken PETER CASSIDY
Chicken with green olives, rosemary and tomatoes DAVID MUNNS
Chicken stuffed with spinach and dates MICHAEL PAUL
Chicken, pancetta and mushroom stew SIAN IRVINE
Paprika chicken with kale and beans MAJA SMEND
Chicken, red onion and mushroom stew LARA HOLMES

MID-WEEK SUPPERS

Roast lemon chicken with three-grain tabbouleh GARETH MORGANS
Moroccan chicken and herb salad DAVID MUNNS
Chicken and almond pilaf MYLES NEW
Yoghurt-spiced chicken with almond rice GARETH MORGANS
Lemon and thyme chicken with roast potatoes and olives MAJA SMEND
Chicken hot wings with blue cheese slaw and skinny fries CLAIRE WINFIELD
Chicken braised with cider and bacon DAVID MUNNS
Pot pie MYLES NEW
Crayfish, chicken and rabbit pie SAM STOWELL
Chicken saltimbocca with green beans and shallots GARETH MORGAN
Chicken Kiev SAM STOWELL
Lemon buttermilk chicken with a piccata sauce GARETH MORGANS
Piri-piri chicken with herb coleslaw DEBI TRELOARS
Chicken and cashew curry with coconut lime noodles DAVID MUNNS

Italian chicken and rosemary stew GARETH MORGANS
Roasted tarragon chicken with carrots, leeks and new potatoes PHILIP WEBB
Soft chicken tacos with black bean salsa DAVID MUNNS
Chicken chilli bowl GARETH MORGANS
Chicken enchiladas ADRIAN LAWRENCE
Budin Azteca LARA HOLMES

ENTERTAINING

Chicken filo parcels with carrot and watercress salad DAVID MUNNS
Chicken and pistachio pilaf MICHAEL PAUL
Prosciutto-wrapped chicken with garlic mash GARETH MORGANS
Fideua with king prawns, chicken and mussels GARETH MORGANS
Baked Spanish rice with chicken and chorizo GARETH MORGANS
Chicken cacciatore DAVID MUNNS
Baked chicken with mascarpone and tarragon MYLES NEW
Chicken with morels, mascarpone and peas PHILIP WEBB
Chicken and purple sprouting broccoli pie DAVID MUNNS
Spicy chicken drumsticks PETER CASSIDY
Tex-Mex chicken with guacamole GARETH MORGANS
Buttermilk fried chicken GARETH MORGANS
Sweet chilli chicken and lime skewers GARETH MORGANS
Roast chicken with peverada sauce GARETH MORGANS
Roast chicken with garlic thyme croutons PETER CASSIDY
Flat-grilled chicken with Texas cornbread ANT DUNCAN
Pot-roast chicken with leeks GARETH MORGANS
Herb-roast chicken PETER CASSIDY
Roast chicken with morels GARETH MORGANS
Slow-roast chicken MYLES NEW

FROM AFAR

Butter chicken curry LARA HOLMES
Chettinad chicken SAM STOWELL
Chicken pasanda GARETH MORGANS
Chicken dhansak with spiced garlic naan CLAIRE WINFIELD
Chicken and butternut curry with cumin and coriander rice SAM STOWELL
Chicken bhuna GARETH MORGANS
West Indian chicken curry MAJA SMEND
Chicken tikka ADRIAN LAWRENCE
Indian-spiced roast chicken MAJA SMEND
Chinese red-braised chicken ANT DUNCAN
Peking-style chicken with spring onion stir-fry LARA HOLMES
Sticky lemon and chilli chicken noodles GARETH MORGANS
Chicken and sweetcorn dumpling soup PHILIP WEBB
Sesame miso chicken with sweet and sour salad GARETH MORGANS
Japanese chicken curry CHARLIE RICHARDS
Yakitori chicken skewers with carrot 'slaw SAM STOWELL
Sesame chicken, pickled red cabbage rice salad ADRIAN LAWRENCE
Bang bang chicken GARETH MORGANS
Thai chicken, cucumber and coconut salad GARETH MORGANS
Quick Thai jungle curry SAM STOWELL
African chicken, sweet potato and peanut curry STUART OVENDEN
Moroccan wings with herb couscous GARETH MORGANS
Jamaican spiced chicken with chargrilled pineapple, rice and peas DAVID MUNNS
Caribbean chicken and black bean stew SAM STOWELL